Madame

GUSTAVE FLAUBERT

Translated by Geoffrey Wall

Level 6

Retold by Christopher Tribble
Series Editors: Andy Hopkins and Jocelyn Potter

Pearson Education Limited
Edinburgh Gate, Harlow,
Essex CM20 2JE, England
and Associated Companies throughout the world.

ISBN: 978-1-4058-6531-9

This translation first published by Penguin UK 1992
First published by Penguin Books 2001
This edition first published 2008

3 5 7 9 10 8 6 4 2

Original translation copyright © Geoffrey Wall 1992
Text copyright © Penguin Books Ltd 2001
This edition copyright © Pearson Education Ltd 2008

Typeset by Graphicraft Ltd, Hong Kong
Set in 11/14pt Bembo
Printed in China
SWTC/02

Published by Pearson Education Ltd in association with
Penguin Books Ltd, both companies being subsidiaries of Pearson Plc

For a complete list of the titles available in the Penguin Readers series please write to your local
Pearson Longman office or to: Penguin Readers Marketing Department, Pearson Education,
Edinburgh Gate, Harlow, Essex CM20 2JE, England.

Contents

Introduction

Deep down in her heart, she was waiting for something to happen. She did not know what it would be, what the wind would blow to her. But every morning when she awoke, she hoped it would come that day. She listened to every sound, watched every new face in the street outside her house for a sign, and could not understand why nothing happened. And then at sunset, sadder than ever, she would long for the next day to come.

Emma Bovary, the wife of a country doctor, finds the reality of her boring marriage impossible to accept. She spends her time reading romantic fiction and staring out of her window, dreaming of a world where she might find the kind of passion and excitement that she reads about in her novels. Her husband, Charles, is a gentle, hard-working man who loves his wife dearly, but he is unaware of her secret desire for escape and adventure.

Her husband's failure to notice her unhappiness makes Emma even unhappier. She loses interest in art and music. She sits for days without speaking. Worried about his wife's mysterious silences and her increasingly frequent illnesses, Charles decides that a change of scene will be good for her. He leaves his successful medical practice in Tostes and moves with his wife to the town of Yonville, not far from Rouen.

On their first night in Yonville, Emma meets a young lawyers' clerk, Léon Dupois. Like her, he is dissatisfied with the dull, mindless life of a small town. For the first time, Emma has met somebody whose company she enjoys. But more than this, a strange feeling of excitement begins to stir inside her – a feeling that at first frightens her but which, in the end, she is powerless to resist...

Madame Bovary is the story of an unfaithful wife, but it is also a revealing study of human desire and an attack on the meaningless rules and attitudes of provincial middle-class society in nineteenth-century France. Gustave Flaubert, the writer, had been born into this kind of his society himself, and he hated it passionately. He had no respect for the middle-class attitudes that surrounded him – the constant thoughts about money, the eager interest in insignificant matters and the meaningless rules of behaviour that had to be obeyed. Flaubert spent his early life attacking this kind of empty, pointless existence. Then, one day, a close friend told him the true story of a country doctor called Eugéne Delamare, who had died of unhappiness after he was deceived and ruined by his wife. The idea for *Madame Bovary* was born, although this was not, as we shall see, the only influence on the book.

Madame Bovary proved to be an exhausting struggle for Flaubert to write. Instead of attacking the middle classes, he was now attempting to write about them in a non-judgemental way. Instead of making fun of the kind of people he most hated, he forced himself to show them talking, thinking and acting in natural ways. He tried to make himself invisible as the tragedy of Emma Bovary slowly unfolded. But the amount of time and effort that he put into accurately detailing the customs of the provincial middle classes clearly suggests Flaubert's true negative opinion of them. Sometimes, the characters in his story made him so angry that he wrote whole scenes about them that were never intended for the final story. This might have wasted valuable time, but it made him feel better and enabled him to return to the real story in a calmer state of mind. Interestingly, however, he seemed to develop a fondness for Emma as the story progressed, and was rarely heard to speak unkindly about her. In fact, he identified with her so much that he made the famous announcement, 'Madame Bovary – c'est moi!' ('Madame Bovary – that's me!')

Another reason why it took five years to write the book was Flaubert's careful search for perfect style. For Flaubert, this was extremely important, and he would spend a long time writing and rewriting every sentence. 'One week – two pages!' he wrote more than once in letters to his friends.

Madame Bovary finally appeared in parts in the *Revue de Paris* in 1856. Flaubert's attention to detail in his powerful description of the psychology and actions of ordinary people has led many people to call *Madame Bovary* a great work of realism. Not surprisingly, however, there were some scenes in the story that shocked many of the magazine's middle-class readers. They were angry, too, about the absence of moral judgement in the book by the author of Emma's behaviour. They complained publicly and the French government brought Flaubert to trial for offending 'public morals and religion'. Flaubert himself was not worried about this. Whatever the result of the case, he had said, his reputation was made. The government lost the case against Flaubert, and *Madame Bovary* became an immediate best seller in book form in April 1857. It is now seen as one of the first modern realistic novels in literature.

Gustave Flaubert was born in Rouen, France in 1821. His father worked at a hospital in Rouen and his mother was a doctor's daughter. Flaubert came into contact with the great doctors of the time and visited hospitals, operating theatres and medical classes. But real life held little attraction for the young Flaubert, and he rebelled by dreaming of strange, foreign lands and reading about history. More importantly, his early unhappiness with provincial life led him to start writing. When he was only thirteen, he wrote to a friend that he would be 'completely disgusted with life' if he were not writing a novel.

His first published work appeared in a small magazine, *Le Colibri*, in 1837. At that time he became friends with the philosopher Alfred le Poittevin, whose pessimistic view of the world had a great influence on him, and his dislike of the accepted ideas of his time increased. He especially grew to hate the middle classes, which, under the rule of King Louis-Philippe, were enjoying a period of increasing power and influence in society.

In 1841, Flaubert became a law student in Paris. At the age of twenty-two he had to give up his studies as a result of a nervous illness, but this enabled him to spend more time on his writing. His father died in January 1846, and his sister Caroline died in March of the following year after giving birth to a daughter. Flaubert retired with his mother and his infant niece to his home at Croisset, near Rouen.

On a visit to Paris in July 1846, Flaubert met the poet Louise Colet. She became his lover, but their relationship did not go smoothly and they separated in 1855. Between 1849 and 1851, he travelled around the Middle East, Italy, Turkey and Greece with a writer friend, Maxime du Camp. Flaubert had already written a novel, *The Temptation of St Anthony*, which was an imaginative, dream-like story influenced by the famous painting by Breughel. Du Camp and another friend, Louis Bouilhet, disliked it, and Bouilhet suggested writing a more realistic novel based on the true story of Eugéne Delamare. The seed for the future *Madame Bovary* was born, but this was not the only source of the story. Another was *The Diary of Mme Ludovica*, an account of the misfortunes of Louise Pradier, the wife of an artist who was also a friend of Flaubert, which is in many ways similar to the story of Emma Bovary.

After the publication of *Madame Bovary*, Flaubert enjoyed fame and success as an intellectual and writer at the court of Napoleon III. Among his friends were the French writers Émile Zola and George Sand, and the Russian writer Turgenev, with whom he shared many of his ideals. But because of his very careful attitude to writing, he took a long time to produce new books, and he only wrote two more novels: *Salammbô* (1862) and *A Sentimental Education* (1869). His early novel, *The Temptation of St Anthony*, which his friends had disliked, was published in 1874, and influenced the early ideas of the young Sigmund Freud. Flaubert did, however, write a number of plays and, towards the end of his life, he published *Trois Contes* (*Three Short Stories*, 1872), which has often been described as his greatest work.

When Flaubert had to give up his own fortune to save his niece's husband from financial disaster, he found happiness only in his work and in the friendship of other writers. He died suddenly in 1880, aged 59, leaving notes for an unfinished novel, *Bouvard and Pecuchet*, in which he returned once again to the subject that had governed his entire life – middle-class stupidity.

Madame Bovary has been made into several films, beginning with Jean Renoir's 1933 version. Perhaps the most famous of them is the 1949 Hollywood film directed by Vincente Minnelli, starring Jennifer Jones and James Mason. In more recent years, there has been a great renewal of interest in the story. Women in particular see Emma as an early heroine of the 'women's movement'. They admire her for her brave, tragic struggle for freedom and her refusal to accept her place and position in a world controlled by men.

Chapter 1   Failure and Success

The older Monsieur* Bovary, Monsieur Charles Denis Bartholomé Bovary, had been a good-looking man when younger, with a big moustache and rings on his fingers. He was not, however, an impressive man, and although he wore expensive clothes, he always looked like an uncomfortable mixture of a military man and a cheap shopkeeper. His good looks and ability to sell himself did, nevertheless, win him a wife with a good income. After he was safely married, he lived for two or three years on her money. He ate and drank well, and spent his days lying in bed till midday, smoking his pipe and never coming home till the theatres and cafés closed.

When his father-in-law died, the old man left very little money to his daughter. Disappointed, Monsieur Bovary tried to start a textile business, but lost a lot of money and finally retired into the country with the idea of showing the people there how to run a farm. However, he knew as little about agriculture as he did about textiles. He rode his horses instead of making them work, ate the fattest chickens instead of selling them, and cleaned his shooting-boots with his own best bacon-fat. He soon discovered that he had little chance of making a fortune.

Around this time he found a place on the borders of Caux and Picardy, half farm, half private house, which he could rent for two hundred francs a year. He took it and there, an angry, disappointed man, at war with the rest of the world, he shut himself up at the age of forty-five. He said that he was disgusted with other people and wanted only to live by himself.

* Monsieur, Madame, Mademoiselle: the French words for Mr, Mrs and Miss. The short forms of Monsieur and Madame are M. and Mme.

At the beginning, his wife had loved him above all others, but this only seemed to add to his dislike of the world and he never had a kind word for her. She had been cheerful, kind-hearted and friendly, but as she grew older, in the same way that good wine turns into vinegar, she became bad-tempered and bad company. She was a hard worker, though, unlike her husband. She was always on her feet, always busy, hurrying to see the lawyers, knowing exactly when the next bills had to be paid. Indoors she was always working: sewing, washing, keeping an eye on the men and paying them their wages. Her lord and master, paying no attention to what was going on around him, sat smoking by the fire.

When the first Madame Bovary had a child, it became the centre of her world. The child's father, however, would have been happy to let him go without shoes. He said that it would be more natural not to give him clothes and to let him run around like a young animal. In contrast to his wife's ideas, he thought a boy would grow up to be a better man if he undressed in the cold, learned to drink alcohol and laughed at the village priest. The child, a gentle little thing, made little progress in this kind of education. His mother always kept him close to her; she cut out pictures for him from the newspaper and made up countless stories. In loving her son, she was looking for something to make up for the loneliness of her life. She dreamed he would be famous. She could see him as a tall, handsome, clever man, high up in the government service. She taught him to read, and to sing – while she played on her old piano. Monsieur Bovary said this was all a waste of time. How were they ever going to afford to educate him for a government job, or help him start in business? Madame Bovary bit her lip and did not argue with her husband, and the child was allowed to run wild in the village.

He went around with the farm workers, scared the birds by throwing stones at them, looked for wild fruit, helped in the fields, wandered through the woods and played with other children. On Saints' days, he helped ring the bells in the church, and he loved to hang on to the big rope and feel himself carried up as it rose in the air. And he grew as strong as a young oak tree, with big hands and red cheeks.

When he reached the age of twelve, his mother managed to arrange for him to begin his studies with the priest, but the lessons were so short and badly organized that they did not do him much good. Sometimes it would be hot and the child would grow tired, and before long the old man would be sleeping with his mouth wide open. At other times the priest would see Charles playing with his friends and would call him over to test his Latin verbs. But then, perhaps, it would begin to rain, or someone they knew would come along, and lessons would be over for that day. The priest always had a good word for his pupil, though, and said that the young man had a very good memory.

By the time young Charles was thirteen, even his father saw that something must be done, and Charles left his unhappy home to spend three unhappy years in the College at Rouen. He wrote to his mother every week; he did his homework. He never did very well in his studies, but he never failed altogether. At the end of three years, his mother took him away from the College, with the plan that he should study medicine.

She got him a room on the fourth floor of a house overlooking a little river. She made arrangements for his meals, found some bits of furniture – a table and a couple of chairs and an old bed – and made sure there was plenty of firewood to keep her poor boy warm. After a week of preparations she went back home, asking him over and over again to look after himself and to study hard.

The list of lectures which he read at the beginning of the term made his head spin. There were lectures on subjects he had never heard of, with names he could not even pronounce. He listened as hard as he could, but he could not understand what the lecturers were talking about. However, he attended every lecture and filled notebook after notebook. He got through his work like a horse that is used to turn a mill-wheel, going round and round in the same place with his eyes covered, never knowing what he was doing or where he was going.

Charles failed his medical examinations the first time – the course was too difficult for him. But his mother still believed in him, and made his father pay for one more year. This time Charles managed to pass and his mother began to plan again. First he must have somewhere to work, and then he must have a wife.

The first problem was solved when the old doctor in Tostes, a small town near Rouen, died. Charles became the next doctor. Then his mother found a 45-year-old widow in Dieppe, with an income of twelve hundred francs a year. Though she was ugly and bad-tempered (and twenty-five years older than Charles), her income made her attractive and Charles thought the marriage would make his life better. He thought he would now have freedom and money to spend. He was wrong. His wife was in charge. She told him what to say, and what not to say. She opened his letters, watched his movements and, when women patients were in the surgery, she listened from the next room. At night, when Charles came to bed, she put her long bony arms round his neck and told him all her troubles. He did not love her, he loved someone else. Yes, she knew she would always be unhappy. And she always ended by asking him for some medicine – and for a little more love.

Chapter 2   Mademoiselle Emma

One night, Charles received a letter asking him to come at once to a farm at Les Bertaux where the farmer had broken his leg. The night was dark and the farm was twenty-five kilometres away, but the farmer was a rich man and Charles was still building up his business. So at four o'clock in the morning, Dr Bovary set out. A child was waiting at an open gate as he approached the farm.

'Are you the doctor?' he asked.

As Charles rode along, he learned from the boy that Monsieur Rouault had broken his leg the night before. He also learned that he had lost his wife two years ago, and had no one with him now except for his daughter, who looked after the house for him.

Mademoiselle Emma, the farmer's daughter, came to the door and showed him into the kitchen. A fire was burning and the men's dinner was cooking in big polished pans. Charles went upstairs to see the farmer. The broken leg was a simple problem and Charles asked the servant and the young woman to help with the patient. As they tied up the farmer's leg, Charles was surprised to see how white her nails were. Her hands, however, were not beautiful – perhaps a little too red. She herself was too tall, and she did not have the kind of soft figure Charles liked. Her good point was her eyes. They were dark, almost black, and she looked at you honestly and fearlessly.

As soon as he had finished looking after his patient, the doctor was invited by Monsieur Rouault to eat before he left. Charles went down into the room below, where two places had been laid with shining silver on a small table and Mademoiselle Emma was waiting for him. A smell of flowers and clean clothes came from a cupboard opposite the window and on the floor, in the corner, stood a few bags of wheat. Someone had hung a drawing of a Greek god in the middle of one of the walls. It was in an attractive frame, and written at the bottom were the words 'To my dear Father'.

They began by talking about Monsieur Rouault, and went on to discuss the weather and the cold winter. Mademoiselle Emma did not like the country very much, especially now she had almost all the responsibility of the farm on her shoulders.

When Charles, who had been upstairs to say goodbye to the farmer, came back into the dining room, he found her standing by the window looking out into the garden. She turned round.

'Are you looking for something?' she asked.

'Yes, I'm trying to find my riding-whip,' he replied, and he began to look behind the doors and under the chairs.

Mademoiselle Emma found it between the bags of wheat and the wall, and Charles went over to help. As he bent down, he felt the young woman's back rubbing against his chest. She stood up, blushing, and, looking at him over her shoulder, handed him his whip.

Instead of going back to Les Bertaux three days later, as he said he would, he returned the next day, and he then went to the farm twice a week. After forty-six days, Monsieur Rouault could move around without help, and people began to say what an excellent doctor Monsieur Bovary was. Père★ Rouault said the very best doctors in Yvetot or Rouen itself could not have treated him better.

Charles did not ask himself why he liked going to Les Bertaux. If he had thought about it he would have said to himself that it was a serious case, or he expected to earn a good fee. But was that really the reason why these visits to the farm were so pleasant? On days when he was visiting, he got up early and rode to the farm as quickly as he could, only stopping to clean his boots and to put on his black gloves before going into the house. He liked to ride into the yard, and see the farm boys as they came forward to meet him. He liked the house, and Monsieur Rouault, who held his hand and said he had saved his life; he liked the sound of Mademoiselle Emma's wooden shoes on the clean stone floor of the kitchen.

★ Père: the French word for father, also sometimes used as a title for an older man.

When he left, she always came with him to the top of the steps, and would wait with him until the boys brought his horse. One day, at the end of the winter, it started to rain as he was leaving the house. She went back inside for an umbrella and put it up. It was a silk one, and it caught the sunlight, reflecting little coloured patches of light on to the whiteness of her skin. She smiled at him, and you could hear the sound of the rain drops as they fell, one by one, on to the tight surface of the silk.

When Charles first began his visits to Les Bertaux, his wife always asked about his patient. But when she learned that the farmer's daughter had been to school and had learned dancing, geography and drawing, and could play the piano, her interest changed to anger and dislike. At first she made unfriendly remarks about Mademoiselle Rouault, but Charles ignored them because he did not want an argument. So at last she told him to his face what she thought of him, and he did not know what to reply. Why did he keep going to Les Bertaux? Monsieur Rouault was well again now and he had not paid his bill. Ah, she knew all about it! There was someone else there, someone who was a good talker, someone who was well educated and clever. That was what he liked – young, pretty ladies!

So Charles agreed to stop his visits to Les Bertaux, but now that he could not see Mademoiselle Emma he decided he could love her. His wife was so unattractive, just skin and bone. She wore the same black clothes and gray stockings, the same ugly shoes all year round. So if he could not see the farmer's daughter any more, he would dream of her!

This unhappy situation lasted for several months until, one fine day in the early spring, the lawyer who had looked after Madame Bovary's affairs left town with all his clients' money. She still had a share in a ship that was worth six thousand francs, and her house in Dieppe, but there was nothing left of that fortune she had been so proud of.

And when her financial affairs were looked into more carefully, Charles's father found out that the house in Dieppe was mortgaged and her share in the vessel was not worth more than two hundred francs. She had lied, the good lady! Monsieur Bovary senior was so angry that he took up a chair and smashed it on the stone floor, and he told his wife she had ruined her son by making him marry an old woman like that. They came to Tostes to tell Charles's rich wife what they thought of her. There was a terrible argument. Heloise begged her husband to defend her against his parents, and Charles did his best, but the old people were still angry when they left the house.

The damage had been done. A week later, as she was hanging out the washing in the yard, Heloise Bovary found that she was spitting blood. The next day, while Charles had his back to her, opening the curtains, she cried out, 'Oh God!' and fell to the floor. She was dead! How amazing!

When the funeral was over, Charles returned to the house. He went up into the bedroom and saw her dress hanging up at the foot of the bed. He stayed there until it was dark, lost in sorrowful thought. After all, perhaps she had loved him.

Chapter 3   A New Wife

One morning Père Rouault came to pay Charles for his treatment, and to say how sorry he was to hear about his wife's death. Seeing how unhappy Charles looked, he said, 'You must make an effort, Monsieur Bovary; you will be happy again one day. Come and see us. My daughter asks about you and says that you are forgetting her. Spring will soon be here. Come and shoot a rabbit or two!'

Charles took his advice. He went back to Les Bertaux, and found everything there just the same as before. The apple trees were already in flower, and Père Rouault did his best to make the doctor feel comfortable. He even told him a few stories, and Charles was surprised to find himself laughing. When he remembered his wife he became serious again, but then the coffee came in and he thought no more about her.

Back home, he also thought of her less and less as he got used to living alone. He was free now to have his meals when he liked, he could go out and come in without having to give explanations, and when he was very tired he could stretch out his arms and legs in bed as far as he liked. He gave himself little treats, let himself feel self-pity and let people be nice to him. Moreover, his wife's death had been rather good for him professionally because, for a whole month, people had been saying, 'Poor young man! What bad luck!' So his name had been heard and his practice had increased and he could go to Les Bertaux whenever he wanted to. He was strangely happy and, looking at himself in the mirror as he brushed his moustache, he thought he had become better-looking.

He arrived at the farm one day at about three o'clock when everyone was out in the fields. He went into the kitchen, but did not see Emma at first. The sunlight shone on the kitchen floor in long narrow bars, reflecting on the ceiling. Flies on the table crawled up the glasses that had not been washed, or drowned in the cider in the bottom of a jug. Between the window and the fireplace Emma sat sewing. She had no scarf around her neck, and he could see the fine hairs on her shoulders.

Like all country people, she offered him a drink. He said no at first, but at last, with a laugh, she persuaded him to have a glass with her. She went to the cupboard and brought out the bottle, took down two small glasses, filled one, poured two or three drops into the other and, tapping it against the doctor's, put it to her lips. As it was nearly empty, she leaned back to drink and, with her head back, she began to laugh because she could not taste anything. At the same time, she tried to catch some of the drops from the bottom of the glass with the tip of her tongue.

Then she sat down and took up her work again – a white cotton sock which she was repairing. She worked with her head bent forward. She did not talk, nor did Charles. As he watched her, the only sound he could hear was the excitement of a hen that had laid an egg in the yard outside.

After some time, Emma started to talk to him. She had been complaining ever since the spring about feeling dizzy; she wondered whether bathing in the sea would do her any good. She began to talk about her convent school, and Charles about his college days. They went upstairs to her room, where she showed him her old music books and the prizes she had won. And she went on to speak of her mother, and even pointed out the bed in the garden where she gathered flowers on the first Friday in every month, to lay on her mother's grave. She said she would like to live in town in the winter, although perhaps the long days made the country even more boring in the summer; and according to what she was saying, her voice was clear and strong, musical or almost a whisper, as if she were speaking to herself.

That night, as he was riding home, Charles thought about the different things she had said, trying to remember them exactly to discover what they meant, so that he might understand how her life had been before he met her. Then he began to wonder how she would become if she married – and whom she would marry. Unfortunately, old Rouault was apparently very wealthy, and she herself . . . so beautiful! But the thought kept coming to him: 'The doctor wants a wife. Yes, the doctor wants a wife.'

That night he could not sleep. He got up, took a drink from the water-jug and opened his window. The sky was filled with stars, a warm breeze was blowing and, a long way off, some dogs were barking. He turned his head towards Les Bertaux. Thinking that, after all, he had nothing to lose by it, Charles made up his mind to ask her to marry him. But every time he was alone with her, the fear of being unable to find the right words left him unable to speak.

In fact Père Rouault would have been happy to see his daughter married, especially as she was very little use in the house. He made excuses for her, telling himself that she had too much intelligence for the farming life. When, therefore, he noticed that Charles blushed each time he was near his daughter, and that the young man was clearly interested in her, he gave the matter some thought. Although Charles was not the sort of man he would have chosen for a son-in-law, he was well educated and a hard worker, and would not ask him for too much money to take his daughter off his hands. This mattered, as Monsieur Rouault had debts with most of his suppliers and had just had to sell a large amount of land.

'If he asks me,' he said to himself, 'he can have her.'

A little later, Charles came to spend three days at Les Bertaux. The time went quickly, and he never seemed to find the right moment to speak. As he was leaving, Monsieur Rouault came out to see him on his way. They had reached a bend in the road and were preparing to say goodbye. It was now or never. Charles gave himself until the corner of the field and at last, when they had passed it, he said, almost in a whisper, 'Monsieur Rouault, there is something I want to say to you.'

They stopped. Charles could not speak.

'Come on then, out with it! Do you think I don't know what it's all about?' said the farmer, laughing quietly.

'Père Rouault . . . Père Rouault . . .'

'Well,' the farmer went on, 'there's nothing I would like better. But, though I am sure my little girl will agree, we must put the question to her. You go on; I'll go back to the farm. If it's yes, there'll be no need for you to come back . . . She'll need some time to get used to the idea! But so you can be sure, I'll open the window in the front bedroom. You'll be able to see it from the back here.'

And with these words he returned to the house.

Charles tied his horse to a tree. He hurried back to take up his position, and waited. Half an hour went by, then nineteen more minutes, which he timed by his watch. Suddenly something banged against the wall. The window was open. She had accepted him!

Next day, by nine o'clock, he was at the farm. Emma blushed when he came in, but tried to laugh a little, too. Père Rouault took his son-in-law in his arms. Then they began to talk about the arrangements. They had plenty of time before them, since the wedding could not take place until at least twelve months after the death of Charles's first wife, and that meant the spring of the following year.

The wedding dinner was a grand affair. Forty-three people sat down at the table and remained there for sixteen hours, and the party which followed went on for several days. For most of the guests it was a wedding to remember. The only person who did not enter the spirit of things seemed to be Madame Bovary senior, who sat through the whole event with a sour look on her face. No one had asked her about the bride's dress, or the arrangements for the party. She went to bed early. Her husband, however, did not follow her, but sent into Saint-Victor for cigars. He sat with the men and smoked until the morning, drinking and laughing until the sun rose.

On the day of the wedding, Charles had not been a great success; he was neither a confident speaker nor a great teller of jokes. Next day, however, he seemed a different man. While Emma did not give the smallest idea of what she thought about it all, Charles was completely changed. He called her his wife, his dear, kept asking where she was, looked for her everywhere and frequently took her out into the yard, where he was seen among the trees with his arm round her waist.

Two days after the wedding, the newly married couple left. Charles could not be away from his practice any longer. Monsieur Rouault sent them home in his carriage, and went with them himself as far as Vassonville. There he kissed his daughter goodbye, and started for home again on foot. When he had gone about a hundred metres he stopped and looked back at the carriage disappearing down the road. Then he thought of his own wedding. Like Charles, he, too, had been happy when he took his wife from her father's house, back to his own. She had ridden behind him through the snow; it was near Christmas and the country all white. One of her arms held on to him, and over the other she carried her basket. When he turned his head he saw close by him, just above his shoulder, her little smiling face. To warm her fingers she had pushed them, from time to time, inside his jacket. How far away it seemed now. He looked back again, and there was nothing to be seen along the road. He felt as sad as an empty house.

Monsieur and Madame Charles arrived at Tostes at about six o'clock. The neighbours came to their windows to take a look at the doctor's new wife. The old servant came to meet them and made excuses for the dinner not being ready, and suggested that, for the moment, Madame should come in and look around the house.

Chapter 4   Two Worlds

The front of the house looked straight on to the street. Hanging up behind the front door were the doctor's coat, a belt, a black leather cap and, on the floor in the corner, a pair of boots covered with dried mud. To the right was the sitting room, where meals were also eaten. White cotton curtains with a red border were hung along the windows, and above the fireplace there was a splendid clock and a head of Hippocrates*. On the other side of the passage was Charles's consulting room, a little box of a place about two metres wide with a table, three ordinary chairs and one armchair. A set of books, the Dictionary of Medical Science, took up almost all the six shelves of the bookcase; they had been owned by many earlier doctors in Tostes, but never read. The smell of cooking would come in through the thin wall during consultations, and anyone in the kitchen could hear the patients coughing and talking to the doctor as clearly as if they were in the room.

The long, narrow garden ran down to the fields. Fruit trees grew along the stone walls and four flower beds, planted with weak-looking roses, were set around a square area which was used for vegetables. At the far end, under some low trees, there was a small white statue of a priest reading a prayer book.

Emma went up to see the bedrooms. There was no furniture in the first one but the second, their bedroom, contained their new bed with its red curtains. There was a box made of seashells on a chest of drawers and on the desk, by the window, stood a glass bottle with a bunch of dried flowers tied with white ribbon. They were the flowers from his first wife's wedding. Charles saw her looking at them, and took them out of the room. Sitting in an armchair, while her maid unpacked her things, Emma thought about her own wedding flowers, lying in one of the boxes, and she wondered what would happen to them if she died young.

Charles was a happy man now. In bed in the morning, with her head on the pillow beside him, he would look at the sunlight

* Hippocrates: an ancient Greek who wrote a moral code for doctors which is still used today.

on her cheek and at her beautiful eyes when she woke. He could lose himself in those eyes, looking into them until he saw a tiny picture of himself, his nightcap on his head and the collar of his shirt open. As soon as he was up and dressed, she would go to the window to see him start his day. Down in the street below, Charles would prepare to get on to his horse while she went on talking to him from above. Sometimes she might find a feather and send it floating through the air to be caught in the long hair on his old white horse's neck. As he rode off, Charles would blow her a kiss and she would wave back to him.

It was the first time in his life that he had tasted such happiness. He had been lonely and friendless at school and when he was studying medicine. And then he had had fourteen months of married life with the widow, whose feet, in bed, were like lumps of ice. But now this lovely woman was his for life!

Before she married, Emma too had thought she was in love, but the happiness that should have come from love was somehow missing. It seemed to her that she must have made a mistake, must have misunderstood things in one way or another. And as she stood by her bedroom window, morning after morning, Emma tried hard to understand what, exactly, the words joy, love, desire meant. They had always seemed so beautiful to her in books, but what did they mean in real life?

Novels had always seemed more real to her than the life she had to live. When she was at her convent school, a teacher sometimes secretly lent such books to the older girls. They were all about love, lovers, beautiful girls, ladies in danger, horses ridden till they dropped dead, dark forests, tears and kisses, and gentlemen as brave as lions. When she was fifteen, Emma read the works of Walter Scott* for the first time and found she was

---

* Walter Scott: a British nineteenth-century writer famous for his historical novels.

happier in this imagined past than her rather boring present; the characters she read about in these books were much more interesting than the teachers and students she saw around her.

She had felt a thrill each time she blew back the thin paper which protected the pictures. She saw young men holding young women in white dresses in their arms, or English ladies with golden hair, who looked at you with big, bright eyes. In her reading she was able to listen to the sound of heavenly music and of falling leaves. Later, after her mother died, she even fell in love with the church and thought of staying in the convent, of never going out into the world. But in her last year of school, she began to lose her interest in religion. When her father took her away, her teachers were not sorry to see her go. She had, they thought, stopped showing any respect for their community.

On her return home, Emma tried to find an interest in managing her father's house, but she soon grew tired of the country and wished herself back in her convent. When Charles came to Les Bertaux for the first time, she thought of herself as a disappointed woman, one for whom life had nothing new to offer, either in knowledge or experience. Maybe her wish for a change – possibly, too, the unrest caused by the presence of an unknown man – had been enough to make her believe that she was at last in love. But now she could not believe that her present state was the happiness she had dreamed about.

Nevertheless, she sometimes thought that these were, in fact, the happiest days of her life. Of course, it would have been so much better if they could have gone far away to lands whose names fall like music on the ear, where the weddings of lovers are followed by mornings of soft delight and where, when the sun goes down, you breathe, sitting beside the sea, the sweet perfume of the lemon trees. Why did her bedroom window not look out on to the Swiss or Scottish mountains? Why did her husband not stand beside her in a black silk jacket, the wind blowing his long hair back from his pale, white forehead?

But Charles could not read these thoughts, and was not able to share her dreams, and as their lives became closer Emma, in fact, began to have a secret feeling of distance from her husband. Charles's conversation was uninteresting to her. He told her that when he lived in Rouen he never had the smallest desire to go to the theatre. He could not swim, he had no idea of how to use a sword, he could not fire a gun. He knew nothing, and he wanted nothing. He thought she was happy, and his heavy, comfortable happiness had begun to annoy her.

A few weeks after they came to Tostes, one of Charles's patients presented Madame with a little Italian hunting dog. She took it with her for walks, because she used to go out sometimes just to get a few moments to herself and to enjoy a change from the garden and the dusty road.

She would go as far as the woods near Banneville, along by the empty summer house at the end of the wall, towards the open country. There, at the side of the lake, the plants grew higher than a man and had leaves as sharp as knives. Sitting at the edge of the wood among the pink and blue wild flowers, her thoughts would wander here and there, like her dog, which ran from one place to the next chasing the birds and insects. But in the same way that her dog always came back to her, she always came back to the same question: 'My God, why did I marry him?'

She would then call Djali (the name she had given her dog) to come to her and, stroking her long, graceful head, would say, 'Come, kiss your mistress; you have no worries, have you?'

Then she would look into the creature's beautiful, sad eyes, and a feeling of tenderness would come over her. Pretending the animal was herself, she would talk to her aloud as if she were comforting someone.

Towards the end of September, however, an extraordinary event happened in her life: she was invited to La Vaubyessard, the home of the Marquis* d'Andervilliers. The Marquis, who had been a Minister in the national government, wanted to get back into politics, and he was now doing his best to make himself popular. During the winter months he had given firewood to the poor, and he was always the first to demand new roads for his district. During the summer, he had had a painful mouth infection, which Charles had managed to cure before it became really serious. The servant who was sent to Tostes to pay for the treatment told his master, when he got back, that he had seen some splendid cherries in the doctor's little garden. Cherries did not grow well at La Vaubyessard, and the Marquis asked Bovary to let him have a few baskets. He then decided to come in person to thank the doctor, saw Emma, and noted that she had a pretty figure and good manners. After this, the Marquis decided that he would not harm his chances in the coming vote if he sent the young people an invitation to his house.

And so, one Wednesday at three o'clock, Monsieur and Madame Bovary set off in their carriage to La Vaubyessard, with a big travelling bag tied on behind, and a hatbox fixed in front. They arrived when it was getting dark, just as the lamps were being lit in the park to guide the carriages. The Château† la Vaubyessard, a large building in sixteenth-century style, stood in the centre of parkland. A stream flowed between tall trees and beneath a bridge, and through the evening mist they could see cottages and farm buildings. Charles stopped the carriage at the foot of the steps leading up to the front door, and two servants came down to take their bags. Then the Marquis came forward and, offering his arm to the doctor's lady, walked with her into the hall.

Under the high ceiling, their voices and footsteps sounded as if

* Marquis, Marquise: the French words for a man of noble birth and his wife.

† Château: the French word for a great house. It can also be used to mean a castle.

they were in a church. As she passed through on her way to the main room, Emma saw large, dark paintings of the Marquis's relatives, some in the clothes of the royal court, others in the uniforms of army or navy officers. When the Marquis opened the door for them, one of the ladies rose (it was the Marquise herself) and came forward to welcome Emma. She made her sit down beside her on a low chair, and began to chat with her, as if she had known her for a long time.

At seven o'clock dinner was served. The men were seated at the first table, in the hall, the ladies at the second, in the dining room, with the Marquis and the Marquise. At the long dining tables, the glasses were filled with iced champagne. Emma felt a thrill go through her as she tasted the coldness of it in her mouth. She had never seen some of the fruit that they had on the table, and even the sugar seemed whiter here, and more finely powdered, than elsewhere.

After dinner, there was dancing. More guests were arriving and the room filled with people. Emma sat down near the door and watched the men talking and smoking cigars in small groups in their black and white evening dress, as the servants moved among them carrying drinks and more small, delicate things to eat. All along the rows of seated women she could see smiles half-hidden, half-revealed, by the flowers the ladies held; everywhere there was silk, the flash of jewels and gold, white arms, and hair piled high on elegant heads.

Emma's heart beat faster when, her partner holding her by the tips of her fingers, she took her place in line and stood waiting for the dance to begin. But her nervousness soon disappeared and, moving to the music, she flew on as light as a bird. The memories of her past life, which until then had always been so clear, disappeared so completely in the magic of the moment that she could hardly persuade herself they were not a dream. There she was. No doubt about that!

During a break in the dancing supper was served, and again the wine flowed freely, accompanied by sea-food soup, sweet puddings and all kinds of cold meats. Now people with longer journeys began to get into their carriages and drive off one after another. Charles was half-asleep with his back against a door. But not everyone was ready to leave, and it was at three in the morning when the last dance began.

Only the guests who were staying the night at the château were still there. One of these, a Viscount whose evening dress fitted him like a glove, came a second time to invite Madame Bovary to dance. They began slowly, and then increased their speed. They turned, and everything around them turned – the lamps, the furniture and the floor. As they swung past the doors, Emma's dress blew up in the air. The Viscount looked down at her, she raised her eyes to his; for a moment she lost her breath and stopped. Then off they went again, quicker than ever, racing down to the high windows at the far end of the room, where she nearly fell and, for a moment, rested her head on his chest. And then, still turning, but more gently now, he took her to her seat. She leaned back against the wall and covered her eyes with her hands. Then there was a little more conversation and, after saying goodnight (or good morning), the guests went off to bed.

Charles dragged himself upstairs on heavy legs. But Emma did not want to sleep. She opened the window and sat with her head in her hand. The night was dark. A few drops of rain were falling. She breathed in the damp wind that blew cool against her eyelids. The dance music was still playing in her ears, and she tried to keep awake in order to keep the dream alive for as long as she could. As she stood there, the sun began to rise beyond the trees and she shivered with cold. She undressed and got down between the sheets, close up to Charles, who was asleep.

There were twelve or fifteen of them at breakfast, which, to Charles's surprise, was all over in ten minutes. After that, a small

20

group went with Mademoiselle d'Andervilliers for a walk through the park, and then, to amuse the lady, the Marquis took Emma to see his stables, while Charles went to ask one of the men to bring his horse and carriage.

When Emma returned, the Bovarys said their goodbyes to the Marquis and Marquise and turned their horse's head towards Tostes and home. Emma sat in silence. Their bags banged against the back of the carriage as they made their way down the rough road. They had reached the high ground at Thibourville when suddenly a group of gentlemen, laughing and smoking cigars, rode past them. Emma thought she recognized the Viscount who had danced with her last night. She turned round to have another look, but they were already too far away.

A little later, they had to stop to make a small repair to the carriage. When he had finished, Charles noticed something lying on the ground between his horse's legs. He bent down and picked up a beautifully-made green silk cigar-case with two cigars still inside it.

'They'll be good this evening after dinner.'

He put the case in his pocket and started the horse.

When they got home, the evening meal was not ready. Madame became angry and the maid, Nastasie, replied rudely.

'You can leave,' said Emma. 'You are finished here!'

So all they had for dinner was onion soup with a small piece of meat and some vegetables.

'How nice it is to be back home again!' said Charles, cheerfully rubbing his hands as he sat down opposite Emma.

They could hear Nastasie weeping as they ate. Charles was rather fond of the poor girl, who had kept him company after his first wife died, when he had nothing to do. She had been his first patient, the first person he ever got to know in Tostes.

'Have you really told her to leave?' he said at last.

'Yes. Why not?' she replied.

After supper, they went into the kitchen to warm themselves while the bedroom was being prepared. Charles began to smoke. He pushed out his lips, spat repeatedly, and pulled his head back every time he breathed in the smoke from the cigar.

'You'll make yourself ill!' she said.

He put the cigar down, and went to get himself a drink of water. Quick as lightning, Emma picked up the cigar-case and threw it into the back of the cupboard.

Time went so slowly the next day! Emma walked around her little garden, up and down, up and down, stopping to look at the flower-beds, at the fruit trees; looking at all these familiar things, things that she knew so well but which now seemed so strange. How far away the château seemed already! Her journey to La Vaubyessard had changed her life, but left it feeling empty. However, she accepted her fate. She folded up her beautiful dress and laid it carefully away in the chest of drawers, with her dancing shoes. She had now known wealth and luxury, and life would never be the same.

The memory of this visit to the château became part of her life. Each Wednesday she would sigh as she awoke and say to herself, 'A week ago today... a fortnight ago... three weeks ago, I was there!' But little by little the faces of the people became faint in her memory, and she forgot the tunes she had danced to. The servants' clothes, the look of the rooms came back less clearly to her vision. Some of the details faded away, but the empty space in her heart remained.

Chapter 5   Moving Home

Often, when Charles was out of the house, Emma would go to the cupboard and take out the green silk cigar-case she had hidden there. It must have belonged to the Viscount. Perhaps it was a present from a lady friend in Paris, made with love and care in every stitch. Paris! What sort of a place was it? 'Paris!' – she said the name under her breath, because she loved the sound of it. It was like the great bell in an old church; the word seemed to add a golden light to everything around it – even to the labels of her little pots of cheap make-up.

She bought a guidebook to Paris and, with her fingertip on the map, she would make little imaginary journeys around the capital. She pretended she was walking along the wide streets, looking in wonder at the great houses. At last, growing tired, she would let her eyes close, and then in the darkness she dreamed she saw the flame of the street lamps, and the steps of the carriages being let down at the entrance to the theatre.

She buried herself in women's magazines, reading every word about opera and fashion and the life of the rich. She read the latest novels – even bringing her book with her to the table and turning the pages while Charles ate and talked. And as she read, the memory of the Viscount came back to her and her dreams became more important, more real to her than her life as a country doctor's wife.

But she tried to improve things in her house. She taught her maid to hand a glass of water held in a white cloth, to knock before entering a room, to dress her mistress. In the daytime, Emma wore a long dress with a silk belt and little red silk shoes. She had bought herself a writing-case, a pen-holder and some envelopes, although she had no one to write to. She thought she would like to travel, or to go back to her school. She wanted to die – and she wanted to go and live in Paris.

And Charles rode from farm to farm on his old horse. He ate breakfast in farmhouse kitchens, visited sick people in their dirty beds, got blood on his hands and face and listened to the last words of the dying. But every night he came home to a fire, a good dinner, a comfortable chair, and a pretty wife who had so many little ways of giving pleasure. It might be paper shades for the candles, a new ribbon for her dress or an extraordinary name for a very ordinary dish, which Charles ate happily, enjoying every bit of it. Everything Emma did added something to the pleasure of his senses and of his home. It was like finding gold-dust in the middle of the narrow pathway of his life.

He felt well, and looked well. People liked him. He talked to their children, did not drink, could be trusted and was especially good with the chest complaints that were so common among country people. A major reason for Charles's success was that he was so afraid of killing his patients that he never gave them anything more than simple medicines – but he was not frightened of surgery, and had a strong wrist when he pulled teeth. The people of the region were happy with their doctor.

Charles did have some ambitions. He tried to read a professional journal after dinner, but the warmth of the room and the good meal he had eaten would send him to sleep after five minutes. And there he sat, his head resting on his two hands and his long hair hanging over his face. Emma looked at him and asked herself why she had not got one of those strong, silent men for a husband, men who sit up at night with their books, and become famous, if not rich. She would have liked the name of Bovary, which was hers now, to be famous, to be seen in the bookshops, talked about in the papers, known all over France. But Charles did not have that kind of ambition, and sometimes she felt like hitting him. 'What a man! What a poor kind of man!' she said to herself, biting her lips.

So as time went on, Emma felt herself less and less able to put up with her husband. He was growing more unpleasant as he got older. He sucked his teeth after eating, and made a horrible noise at every mouthful of soup he swallowed. As he was beginning to put on weight, his eyes, which were already small, looked as if they would start to disappear into his increasingly fat face.

Deep down in her heart, she was waiting for something to happen. She did not know what it would be, what the wind would blow to her. But every morning when she awoke, she hoped it would come that day. She listened to every sound, watched every new face in the street outside her house for a sign, and could not understand why nothing happened. And then at sunset, sadder than ever, she would long for the next day to come.

The spring came again. With the first touch of heat, when the apple trees were in flower, she began to have attacks of dizziness. And when July came, she counted on her fingers how many weeks it would be to October, thinking that perhaps the Marquis d'Andervilliers would be giving another dance at La Vaubyessard. But September came and went, and no one called or wrote.

After this disappointment there was the same emptiness in her heart, and the empty days began again as before. The future was like a corridor in which there was no light, and at the end of it only a closed door. She gave up her music. What was the use of playing? Who was there to hear? She stopped her drawing. What was the good, what was the good of it all? Even sewing bored her.

'There's nothing left to read,' she said to herself. And there she sat, staring at the falling rain.

Was this hopeless life going to last for ever? Was there no escape? She knew she was just as good as the luckier ones. At La Vaubyessard she had seen great ladies who were not as pretty or intelligent as her; why was she so unlucky? She would lean her head against the wall and weep, wanting so much for a life of excitement, pleasures, all the delights which must be out there in the world, but which were not hers. There were days when she would talk and talk; then the excitement would die away, and she would fall back into a kind of dream world and sit without moving or saying a word.

As she was always saying how she hated Tostes, Charles thought her illness must be caused by the place itself. The idea grew on him, and he began seriously to think of going elsewhere. Then she started drinking vinegar to make herself lose weight, coughed a little dry cough and could not touch her food.

It was hard for Charles to leave Tostes. He had been there for four years and was building a good practice. However, what must be must be. He took her to Rouen to see another doctor. The doctor said it was a case of nerves. What she needed was a change. So Charles looked around all over the place, and at last heard of a busy little market town called Yonville-l'Abbaye, somewhere in the Neufchâtel area, where the doctor had recently left town and no replacement had been found. He wrote to the local pharmacist asking him to let him know how many people there were in the place, what sort of competition there was, and how much a year the other man used to make. The answers were satisfactory, and Charles decided he would make a move in the spring if Emma's health had not improved.

One day, when she was emptying a drawer in preparation for the move, Emma felt something sharp against her finger. It was the piece of wire around her wedding flowers, faded and dusty now, and the ribbon eaten by insects. She threw them on the fire, where they burned like a handful of dry grass and then lay like a red bush in the fireplace. As she watched them burn, the paper berries burst, the wire bent and twisted, and the paper flowers were held in the hot air like black insects until, at last, they flew up the chimney.

In March, when they left Tostes, Madame Bovary was pregnant.

Chapter 6   Yonville

Yonville-l'Abbaye is a market town about twenty-six kilometres from Rouen, between the Abbeville and Beauvais roads. It is on the borders of Normandy, Picardy and the Ile-de-France, the sort of place where the language has no accent and the landscape no character. Here they make the worst cheese in the whole district, and farming is expensive because the sandy, stony soil is so poor.

Until 1835 there was no good road to Yonville, and although a new one has been built, nothing has really changed there for a hundred years. Walking into the town you still pass small farmhouses set in their own gardens, and see that the fields stretch almost into the centre of the town. The market, with its red roof supported by twenty or more wooden posts, takes up half of the town square. The Town Hall is a large, important-looking building, but what really catches the eye is the pharmacy of Monsieur Homais just opposite the town's one hotel, the Lion d'Or.

The pharmacy is especially attractive at night when the lamps are lit and the big red and green glass bottles in the window send long beams of coloured light far out along the ground. From top to bottom, the building is covered with advertisements for medicines and mineral water, and the shop-sign which goes right across the front carries in golden letters the words 'Homais, Pharmacist'. At the far end of the shop, the word 'Laboratory' appears over a glass door on which, halfway up, the name 'Homais' is repeated in more gold letters on black.

And that is all there is worth seeing in Yonville. The one and only street, with a shop or two on either side of it, stops at the bend in the road. If you turn to your right and follow the path at the foot of the hill, you come to the cemetery.

The night the Bovarys arrived in Yonville, Madame Lefrançois, who ran the inn, was so busy that the sweat ran down her face as she rushed around among her pots and pans. Tomorrow was market day and she still had the meat to cook, the soup to make and the coffee to get ready. Then there was the meal for her regular customers, as well as for the new doctor and his wife and maid – whose coach was now half an hour late.

27

Shouts of laughter came from the bar, where three workmen were calling for more wine and the wood fire was burning. A man in soft green leather shoes, a smoking cap on his head, was standing warming his back by the fire. He had a look of complete self-satisfaction on his face, and he appeared to be as carefree as the small bird in the cage which hung from the ceiling. It was the pharmacist, waiting for the evening meal which he regularly ate at the hotel.

He did not have to wait too long. Soon, Madame Lefrançois heard the sound of wheels and the metal shoes of a tired horse on the road outside.

As soon as the coach stopped, other villagers came to the inn, and all began to speak at once, asking for news, explanations and packages they had been waiting for. As he gave out his parcels, Hivert, the coachman, told them they had been delayed because Madame Bovary's little dog had run away and had not been found.

Emma had, in fact, been crying for the last hour. She said it was Charles's fault. Monsieur Lheureux, who was travelling inside the coach and who had the fabric shop in the village, had done his best to make her happier by telling her of several cases in which dogs had come back to their masters after years of separation. There was a story, he said, of a dog that found its way back to Paris all the way from Constantinople!

Dog or no dog, they had arrived at their new home, and had to leave the coach. Emma got out first, then Félicité, her maid, and then Monsieur Lheureux. They had to wake Charles up; he had fallen asleep in his corner as soon as it grew dark.

Homais introduced himself, offered his services to Madame and his respects to Monsieur, told them he was charmed to have been able to do them a service, adding with a smile that he had invited himself to dinner as his wife was away from home.

As soon as she was in the kitchen, Madame Bovary went over to the fire. With the tips of two fingers she took hold of her dress at the knee and, raising it above her ankles, stretched out a foot to the flames – a little foot in a black boot. The fire lit her from top to toe, its red light making her dress shine and showing the perfect white skin of her face. On the other side of the fireplace, a fair-haired young man watched her in silence.

Monsieur Léon Dupuis, clerk to the town's only lawyer, also ate regularly at the Lion d'Or. As he found life in Yonville almost impossibly boring, he would often delay his meal in the hope that a traveller would arrive at the inn with whom he could enjoy a conversation in the evening. It was therefore with some pleasure that he accepted the suggestion that he should sit down with the Bovarys.

At the table, Homais asked permission to keep on his cap, for fear of catching cold.

'Madame must be a little tired,' he said, turning to Emma. 'It is not a comfortable journey.'

'Very true,' she answered, 'but I love moving around. I hate staying in one place.'

'Oh, I agree. Staying in one place is horrible!' said the clerk.

'But if you were like me,' said Charles, 'and always had to be on your horse . . .'

And so the meal continued. Charles spent most of his time discussing medical matters with Monsieur Homais, while Léon told Madame Bovary about the attractions of the neighbourhood. They quickly discovered that they shared the same romantic tastes.

'I think there's nothing so beautiful as a sunset, especially by the sea!' said Madame Bovary.

'Oh, I love the sea!' Monsieur Léon replied.

'And doesn't it seem to you, somehow, that you think more freely, and that it raises your soul and makes you think of the endless nature of things?'

'It's just the same where there are mountains,' Léon went on.

So they continued talking of Switzerland and Italy, which they had never visited, and music, which neither of them could play, and reading – the one thing that both of them did enthusiastically.

'What can be better than sitting by the fire in the evening with a book, when the lamp is lit and the wind beats against the window?' said Léon.

'That's just what I think,' she replied, looking at him with her big, dark eyes.

'You forget everything,' he went on. 'The hours slip by. Sitting still in your armchair, you can wander in strange places and imagine they are there before your eyes.'

'Oh yes, that's true!' she said.

They had been at the table for two and a half hours by now, since Artemise, the servant, did not hurry as she brought the dishes in from the kitchen. Quite unconsciously, Léon had put his foot up on one of the bars of the chair on which Madame Bovary was sitting, moving closer so he could catch everything she said. And so, while Charles and the pharmacist went on with their discussion, Emma and Léon sat close to one another, and entered into a conversation in which they talked about the interests they shared: the Paris theatres, names of novels, the latest dances, the world of fashion, which neither of them knew anything about, Tostes, where she had lived, and Yonville, where they were now. They discussed anything and everything, and talked all through dinner.

When the coffee was brought in, Félicité went to arrange the bedroom in the new house, and the group around the dinner table soon afterwards rose to go. Madame Lefrançois had fallen asleep by the dying fire, while the manservant, lamp in hand, was waiting to show Monsieur and Madame Bovary to their house.

The house felt damp and cold after the warmth of the inn. The walls were new and the wooden stairs had no carpet. Upstairs in the bedroom, a pale light came in through the curtainless windows. The tops of some trees could just be seen, and beyond them, the fields in the moonlight.

This would be the fourth time Emma had slept in a new bedroom. The first was when she went to the convent, the second when she came to Tostes, the third at La Vaubyessard, and now this was the fourth. And every time, it had seemed as if she were entering a new stage in her life. She could not believe that things would look and be the same in different places. The most recent period of her life had been bad, so the next part would have to be better.

Chapter 7   In Love

Next morning, when she awoke, Emma saw the clerk walking across the square. She was in her dressing-gown. He looked up and took off his hat. She gave a little nod and quickly shut the window.

All day long, Léon waited for six o'clock to arrive. But when he went round to the inn, the only person there was Monsieur Binet, the tax collector, already seated at the table. The dinner of the night before had been an important event for Léon. It was the first time in his life that he had talked to a woman for a whole evening. How did he manage to tell her, and in such brilliant language, so many things he could not have expressed so well before? Unfortunately, it did not look as if he would have the chance to repeat his performance for the moment.

Monsieur Homais, the pharmacist, however, was able to visit Madame Bovary and show what a good neighbour he was. He told her all about the shopkeepers, where to get her butter cheaply, and he helped her find a gardener. It has to be said, however, that he was not doing this out of pure kindness. Monsieur Homais had, a year earlier, broken the law which forbade the practice of medicine by all unqualified persons. Someone had told the authorities, and Monsieur Homais had been given a very severe warning by the magistrate in Rouen. The problem was that he still liked to give quick, innocent consultations in his shop, but the Mayor did not like him, others were jealous, and he was playing a dangerous game. So Monsieur Homais thought to himself that if he did things for Monsieur and Madame Bovary, Monsieur Bovary would be grateful, and a grateful man does not make complaints to the authorities in Rouen.

Every morning, Homais would come across with the newspaper and often, during the afternoon, he would leave his shop for a minute or two to chat with the new doctor. Charles was not a happy man; patients did not come. He sat for hour after hour in silence, or he went to sleep in his surgery or watched his wife sew. He even started doing some small jobs at home, trying to paint the bedroom with some paint the men had left behind. Money was his great worry. He had spent such a lot on repairs at Tostes, on his wife's clothes and on moving, and most of his savings and Emma's money had gone in two years.

But Charles also had something pleasant to think about, as his wife was expecting a child, and the closer they got to the time, the more loving he became. It was another link between them, real evidence of their marriage. When he watched her heavier walk, when she sat opposite him at the table, or when she was in her armchair after dinner, he could not stop himself getting up, kissing her, stroking her face, calling her 'little mother'. The idea of being a father pleased him very much. He lacked nothing.

At first Emma was surprised by his attention; then all she wanted was to have the baby as soon as possible, so that she would know how it felt to be a mother. Their shortage of money meant that she could not buy all the things she wanted for the new arrival, so perhaps she did not feel as much love for the child she carried as she wanted to give. But she thought about it all the time.

She hoped it would be a boy. He should be strong and dark, and they would call him George. And the thought of having a boy somehow made her feel better. A man would be free, while a woman is always limited. She is weaker and economically dependent, and the habits of society do not permit her the same freedom.

Emma's baby was born on a Sunday morning at about six, just as the sun was rising.

'It's a girl,' said Charles.

She turned away her head and fainted.

Madame Homais came to the house as soon as the news was given to congratulate her, and so did Madame Lefrançois of the Lion d'Or. The pharmacist offered his congratulations through the half-open door. He then asked to see the baby and declared it was the most well formed he had ever seen.

As the doctor felt that his wife was not strong enough to feed the baby herself, the little girl was sent to a wet nurse. With nothing else to do in the days after the birth, Emma tried to think of a name for her daughter. First she went through names with Italian endings, like Clara, Louisa, Amanda. She rather liked old names like Galsuinde, or Yseult or Léocadie. Charles wanted the child to be called after her mother. Emma said no.

At last Emma remembered that at the Château de la Vaubyessard she had heard the Marquise call a young woman by the name of Berthe. That decision was made.

Four or five weeks after the birth, Emma felt a sudden need to see her little girl, so she set out in the direction of the wet nurse's house at the far end of the village. It was midday and the sun beat down from a cloudless sky. A hot wind was blowing and when she had gone some way, Emma began to feel weak from the effort of walking. She started to think she should return home or go in somewhere and sit down.

Just then, Monsieur Léon came out from a house close by,

with some papers under his arm. He came up and spoke, and took her into the shade outside Lheureux's shop. Madame Bovary said she was on her way to see her baby, but that she was beginning to feel tired.

'If . . .' began Léon, but he stopped, not daring to continue.

'Are you very busy?' she asked.

And when the clerk said that he was not, she begged him to walk with her.

To reach the nurse's house they had to go along to the end of the street and then turn, as if they were going to the cemetery. They set off side by side, and recognized the house by an old tree that shaded it. It was a low, badly maintained house with a brown roof and small, untidy garden.

Hearing the gate open, the woman came out, carrying a baby at her breast. With her other hand she was dragging along a poor, miserable-looking two-year-old with spots all over his face.

'Come in,' she said. 'Your little one is in there asleep.'

She went into the dark bedroom, and showed Emma where the little girl was sleeping. Emma took the baby in her arms, wrapped up in a dirty blanket, and began to sing gently as she held her.

Léon walked up and down the room. It seemed strange to him to see this beautiful, elegantly dressed woman in such poor surroundings. Madame Bovary saw him looking and blushed bright red. He turned away, thinking he had perhaps seemed too curious, as she gave the baby back to the nurse. It had just been sick all over her collar.

Having lost enthusiasm for her baby, Emma again took Monsieur Léon's arm, and they left the nurse holding the child and waving as they went down the path. Emma walked quickly for some distance, then slowed down. As she looked around her, her eyes rested on the young man's shoulder and on his well-cut coat with its smart black collar. She noticed how his golden

34

brown hair was smooth and carefully brushed, and that his fingernails were longer and much more carefully cared for than most fingernails in Yonville.

They went back to the village on the path beside the river. The stream flowed on noiselessly, deep and cool; dark plants moved in the water like long green hair, and insects walked over its smooth surface or waited with shining wings on the tall grass at the water's edge. All around, as far as the eye could see, the fields had emptied of people. It was dinner-time in the farms, and the only sounds that fell on the ears of the young woman and her companion were their footsteps on the path, the words they spoke and Emma's dress brushing against the grass. The garden walls were hot in the sun, and the wild plants that were growing between the stones had died. As she passed, Madame Bovary touched some of their dry flowers, which made them fall into yellow dust.

They were talking about some Spanish dancers who were going to perform at the theatre in Rouen.

'Will you go?' she asked.

'If I can,' he replied.

Was this all they had to say to one another? They tried to speak of ordinary, everyday things, but all the time they felt a deep change coming over them. It was like a whisper from the soul, deep down, stronger than the spoken word. Lost in wonder at this strange sweetness, they did not speak of it or try to explain what was happening. But both felt that there could be future pleasures waiting for them.

When they came to her garden, Madame Bovary pushed open the little gate and, running up the steps, disappeared from view.

Léon went back to his office. His boss was out. He looked quickly at some papers, prepared a pen for writing, but then put on his hat and went out. He went up to the edge of the woods, threw himself down on the ground under the trees and looked at the sky through his fingers.

'Oh!' he sighed. 'I am so bored!'

As soon as the weather began to turn cold, Emma spent her days in the sitting room. It was a long room with a low ceiling, and above the fireplace there was a picture of the sea and a large mirror. She pulled her chair close to the window so that she could watch the villagers as they went by on the pavement.

Twice a day, Léon passed from his work to the Lion d'Or. Emma could recognize his steps from a long way away. She leaned forward and listened, and the young man walked past, always dressed the same and always looking straight in front of him. In the evening, when she had dropped her piece of unfinished sewing on her lap and was sitting with her chin resting on her left hand, she would again notice his figure moving past the window, and then she would get up and tell the girl to lay the table for dinner.

Monsieur Homais would often come in while they were eating. Smoking cap in hand, he would come in quietly, not wanting to disturb anyone, and always saying the same thing: 'Good evening, everybody.' Having taken his usual place at the table, between husband and wife, he asked the doctor about his patients, and the doctor consulted him about the sort of fees he ought to charge. Then they began to discuss the news in the paper. At eight o'clock the pharmacist's assistant, Justin, would come for him to go over and shut up the shop.

On Sundays, the Bovarys would return these visits and spend the evening at the pharmacist's. They would begin with cards – Monsieur Homais usually being Emma's partner. Léon would stand behind her and tell her what to play. Every time she threw a card on the table, the movement would pull up her dress on the right side, and her hair would move across her neck like soft brown silk.

When they had finished the cards, the pharmacist and the doctor would settle down to discuss the news of the day and drink their wine and Emma, changing her place, would sit with her elbow on the table, turning over the pages of an illustrated magazine. Léon sat down beside her, and they looked at the pictures together, waiting for each other at the bottom of the page. Sometimes she would ask him to read some poetry. And so a kind of friendship began between them.

The problem for Léon, however, was to know what sort of friend Madame Bovary might be. They gave each other small presents, they were happy in each other's company, but would there be more? He thought and thought about this in his lonely room. Should he tell her what he was feeling? Did he love her, or didn't he? He was torn between fear of hurting her and shame at his own lack of courage. Sometimes he would make up his mind to act, and to act quickly. He wrote letters – and tore them up; decided on a day to speak to her – and put it off. Sometimes he walked out of the lawyer's office with his mind made up. But all his courage melted when he found himself face to face with Emma; and when Charles came home and invited him to come with him to see a patient at a farm a few kilometres away, he at once accepted and, with a bow to Madame, left with her husband.

But Emma did not ask herself if she was in love. Love, she thought, was something that must come suddenly, like a great thunderstorm, blowing away your old life and carrying your heart and soul away, to heaven or to hell. She never thought about the way a river can rise slowly, getting higher day by day, until after a night of rain it breaks its banks and floods the land around it. In fact, she had no idea of the danger she was in.

Chapter 8   A Dream Ends

One snowy Sunday afternoon in February, Monsieur and Madame Bovary, Homais and Monsieur Léon went to look at a new mill that was being built outside Yonville. Homais had brought his children, to give them a little exercise. The place did not interest Emma, and she stood away from the group, leaning on Léon's arm, while Homais and her husband talked about the technical wonders – the thick walls, the great machinery – they saw all around them.

Turning from the pale sunlight coming through the mist, she saw Charles, his cap pulled down over his ears, his thick lips and his stupid face. Even his back was annoying, a stupid back covered in a stupid, boring winter coat. Léon moved forward a step. The cold air had made him pale, even more beautiful than normal. The collar of his shirt was open a little, showing his white skin; the tip of his ear was visible under his long hair, and his big blue eyes, raised upwards to the clouds, seemed to Emma to be clearer, more beautiful than those mountain lakes in which the skies are mirrored.

Madame Bovary did not go over to her neighbours' that evening, and when Charles had left and she felt she was all alone, she lay down on the carpet in front of the fire and thought about Léon once more. She thought he was charming. She could not put him out of her thoughts. She remembered how he had stood, the things he had said, all about him. And she said over and over again, 'Oh, charming! Charming! . . . And in love?' she asked herself. 'But with whom? . . . But it must be with me!'

The evidence was suddenly clear to her and her heart gave a great leap. The firelight became brighter, and she turned on her back and stretched out her arms.

After the first excitement, she then thought, as so many people have before, 'Ah, why did this happen when it was too late? Why not before? What prevented it?'

It was midnight when Charles got back. She pretended she had just woken up and, as he made a noise undressing, she complained of having a headache. Then she asked what sort of an evening it had been.

'Monsieur Léon,' he said, 'went to bed early.'

She could not help smiling. When she turned over to go to sleep, her heart was filled with a new happiness.

Next day, however, she could not settle to her work in the house; she was happy, but still could not take pleasure in the things she usually liked to do. So when Monsieur Lheureux, the draper, visited and showed her a beautiful scarf, even offering to let her pay later, she refused. And when Léon visited her in the afternoon, all she could do was to talk about her husband!

The same sort of thing went on for days. Her manner and conversation changed completely. She became interested in housekeeping, started going to church again regularly, and stopped the cook stealing the sugar. She even took her little daughter Berthe away from the wet nurse and showed her to all her visitors. She told everyone she loved children. They were such a joy and comfort, she said, as she kissed the child and held her close to her. When Charles got home, he would find his chair ready by the fire. His clothes were brushed and cleaned, the buttons were always on his shirts, and his shirts were folded carefully after they had been ironed. When Léon saw him at the fireside after dinner, with his hands on his stomach, his cheeks red from the meat and wine, the child crawling around on the carpet, and this elegant woman who would lean over and kiss him over the back of the chair, he would say to himself, 'What a fool I am to imagine I could make her care for me!'

And as each day passed, Emma became thinner and paler. She was so sad and so calm, so gentle and, at the same time, so distant, that you felt a sort of icy charm when you were with her. This charm changed the attitudes of her neighbours; they no longer saw her as the outsider who did not know how to behave properly.

'She's a wonderful woman,' said the pharmacist, and the married women of Yonville admired her for her good management, the patients for her pleasant manners, the poor for her charity. But beneath her calm, Emma was in a state of desire and anger and hatred. Her plain, simple dress hid a heart that was breaking, and she could tell no one, no one! She was in love with Léon, but she did not want to see him. Her heart beat faster when she heard him coming, and then, when he was there, the excitement went away and was replaced by a feeling of fear and sadness. She did not know what to do.

What made it harder to bear was that Charles had no understanding of what she was going through, and she began to hate him for his lack of feeling. She would have liked Charles to beat her so that she could have a reason for hating him. She was torn between a love she could not admit to, and a hatred she could not show. And there she sat at the end of another empty day, broken, motionless, her face wet with tears.

'Why don't you tell the doctor about it?' said her maid when she came in and found her like this.

'It's only nerves,' answered Emma. 'Don't mention it to him. He would only worry.'

If Emma was unhappy, Léon was also less than pleased with his life, feeling he had nothing to look forward to. He was so tired of Yonville and its inhabitants that the sight of certain people and certain houses made him angry. And when Monsieur Homais, the pharmacist, tried to amuse him, he found himself disliking him too. The problem was, however, that the thought of changing things alarmed him as much as it excited him.

And the more he thought about it all, the more impatient he became. 'Paris' was the word he kept saying to himself. Since he had to go there for his final examinations, why not go now? What was stopping him? And he began to plan a new life for himself. He would live like an artist. He would take guitar lessons. He would wear a red coat and a blue hat; he would go to the opera every night and drink wine with actresses! The great difficulty would be to persuade his mother to agree – but, in fact, it was quite easy. His own employer had been telling him to take up work in another office and widen his experience, and his mother wanted Léon to qualify as soon as possible. Two days after he had sent his letter, she wrote back to him giving her permission!

When he knew he could leave, however, he did not hurry. Every day, for a whole month, boxes and parcels were delivered to his rooms in Yonville; and although Léon had soon made enough preparations – and more than enough – for a voyage round the world, he kept putting things off from week to week.

However, at last the time came to leave, and he hardly had time to say goodbye to Monsieur Bovary. He ran up the stairs to the sitting room, and as he went in Madame Bovary rose quickly.

'Here I am again!' said Léon.

'I knew you would come!'

She bit her lip hard, and could feel herself blush from the roots of her hair to the edge of her collar. She remained standing, leaning her shoulder against the wall.

'Is the doctor in?' he said.

'No, he's gone out.' And she repeated, 'He's gone out.'

Then there was silence.

'I would like to kiss Berthe goodbye,' he said.

Emma went down a few stairs and called Félicité.

He gave a long look round – at the walls, the shelves, the fireplace – as if to carry the memory of it away with him.

Emma returned, and the servant came in with Berthe. Léon kissed her several times on the neck.

'Goodbye, my poor little thing; goodbye, my darling, goodbye.' And he gave her back to her mother.

'Take her away,' she said.

And now they were alone.

Madame Bovary had her back to him, her face against the glass of the window. Léon was holding his cap in his hand and beating it gently against his thigh.

'It's going to rain,' said Emma.

'I've got a coat,' he answered.

'Ah!'

She turned away again, her face down. No one could have said what Emma was looking at through the glass.

'Well, this is goodbye!' he sighed.

She raised her head with a sudden movement.

'Yes, goodbye . . . Oh, go!'

They advanced towards each other. He held out his hand. She hesitated. 'In the English style, then!' she said, putting hers in his, forcing herself to laugh.

Léon felt her hand between his fingers, and it seemed that his whole life flowed into it.

Then he released her hand, their eyes met for a moment, and he was gone.

Chapter 9   Starting Again

The next day, for Emma, was like a funeral. She felt the same grey unhappiness she had known when she came back from La Vaubyessard with the dance tunes playing in her head and her boring husband sitting opposite her. In her imagination, Léon came back to her, taller, more beautiful than ever; though he was separated from her, he had not left her. He was there, and the walls of the house seemed to hold his shadow. She asked herself again and again why she had not taken the chance when it was offered to her. Why hadn't she held him back with both hands, begged and prayed to him on her knees, when he tried to leave? She cursed herself for not giving her love to Léon; she was thirsty for his lips. She wanted to fly after him and join him, to throw herself into his arms and say, 'I have come, I am yours!' But Emma was afraid of all the difficulties in the way; she wanted Léon and dared not give herself, and her desire seemed to grow day by day.

And so the memory of Léon became the centre of her sorrow. It shone in the darkness, and she hurried towards it to warm herself by the dying flames. But the fires died down and, little by little, the flame of love cooled. Then the unhappy days of Tostes began all over again, but she felt herself much more unfortunate now; she had experience of grief, and she knew with certainty that it would never end.

A woman who has given up as much as she had, had the right to a few luxuries. In a single month, she bought fourteen francs' worth of lemons to clean her nails. She wrote to Rouen and ordered a blue silk dress, and from Lheureux she bought the finest scarf he had in his shop. She tied it round her waist, outside her dressing-gown, and would lie by the hour on the sofa with the curtains closed and a book in her hand.

But despite her little comforts, Emma did not become happy. She had that tight look at the corners of her mouth which you see in people who have failed in their lives. She was pale, white as a sheet, and she had an uncertain, hunted look in her eyes. And because she had discovered three grey hairs, she talked about being an old woman. Also, she had frequent attacks of dizziness. One day she spat blood and, as Charles rushed over to her, obviously very anxious, all she said was, 'Bah! What does it matter?' Charles went and shut himself in the surgery and wept.

Although the Bovary household had become a place of unhappiness again, life in Yonville continued as usual. People went to the church on Sundays, and on Wednesdays the market was held in the town square. From early morning the square filled up with farmers and people with goods to sell from as far as Rouen.

On Wednesdays the pharmacy never emptied. Some came to buy medicine, others to get advice. Monsieur Homais was a well-known man in all the villages near Yonville, and they thought he knew more about doctoring than all the doctors put together. Emma was seated at her window and was amusing herself by looking at the crowd of country people, when she noticed a gentleman in a green coat. He was wearing yellow gloves and heavy, highly polished brown leather boots, and was making his way towards the doctor's house, followed by a farm worker.

'Can I see the doctor?' he asked the maid. 'Tell him Monsieur Rodolphe Boulanger of La Huchette is here.'

Charles came into the room, and Monsieur Boulanger presented his man, who said he wanted to be bled to cure his dizziness. So Bovary told them to bring him a bandage and a basin, and asked the maid to hold it.

'Don't be afraid,' he said, turning to the farm worker, who had gone as white as a sheet.

'Not me, sir!' he replied. And he stuck out a great arm for Charles to cut, and out shot the blood.

'Hold the bowl nearer!' cried Charles.

'Look!' said the worker. 'You'd think it was a little fountain. My blood's red enough! You'd say that was a good sign now, wouldn't you?'

'Sometimes they feel nothing to start with. Then faintness begins, especially with big, strong people like this man here,' said Charles to Monsieur Boulanger.

Hearing this, the man gave a sudden movement and fell back into the chair.

'I knew it!' said Bovary, putting his finger on the vein. But now the bowl of blood was beginning to shake in the maid's hands, and she also turned pale.

'Emma! Quick! I want you!' shouted Charles.

She ran down the stairs.

'Get me some vinegar,' he said. 'Good Lord, two of them at once!'

'It's nothing at all,' said Monsieur Boulanger calmly, as he took the maid in his arms and leaned her against the wall.

Madame Bovary took hold of the basin. She bent down to put it under the table, and as she did so her long yellow dress spread out all around her on the floor. Then, as she stretched out her arm, she swayed a little and the cloth moved with her, following the shape of the body beneath it. After a moment she went to fetch a jug of water, and she was putting some pieces of sugar in it when the pharmacist arrived to see what was happening.

When things had become calmer, they began to talk about fainting attacks. Madame Bovary said she had never had one herself.

'That's unusual for a woman,' commented Monsieur Boulanger. 'But there are some sensitive people around. I have seen soldiers faint at the sound of the big guns being prepared.' Emma listened to him with admiration in her eyes. 'Anyway, my man's fainting has given me the pleasure of meeting Madame,' he added, looking at Emma as he spoke.

He put down three francs on the corner of the table, bowed and departed. He was soon on the other side of the river, on the road back to La Huchette, and from the bedroom window Emma could see him slowing down from time to time, like someone lost in thought.

'Pretty little woman, this doctor's wife – very pretty indeed! Lovely teeth, dark eyes, neat foot. She could be a Parisian. Where does she come from, and where did our fat country doctor pick her up?' Monsieur Rodolphe Boulanger was a man of thirty-four, hard-hearted but clever. He had plenty of experience with women, and knew how to get on with them. This latest one had attracted his attention. 'The doctor looks a dull dog to me. I expect she's sick of him. He's got dirty nails and three days' beard. While he's out seeing his patients, she sits at home mending socks. And she's sick to death of it, wants to live in town and go to a dance every night. Poor little woman! She's dying for love. A word or two about hearts and flowers and she'd be at your feet. But getting rid of her afterwards, that's where the trouble would come in.'

There was no one around, and the only sounds Rodolphe heard were the grass brushing against his boots and the cry of the insects in the fields. Once more he imagined Emma, dressed as he had seen her, and he started to undress her in his mind.

'Oh, I'll have her!' he cried, striking out at the earth with his stick.

Two weeks later it was the day of the famous Yonville Agricultural Show, the most important event of the year. On the morning of the great day, the inhabitants were all out on their doorsteps discussing the arrangements. The front of the Town Hall had been decorated, a tent had been put up for the lunch, and the whole town was alive with activity.

The crowd poured into the High Street from both ends of the village. What caused the greatest admiration were two tall poles covered with tiny lamps, standing beside the platform where the most important guests would sit. Madame Lefrançois, the landlady of the Lion d'Or, and Monsieur Homais, the pharmacist, stood on the steps of the hotel watching the growing crowd and the men going in and out of the Café de France – the main competition to the Lion d'Or.

'Well, that won't last much longer,' she said. 'One more week and that will be the end of it.'

Homais looked at her in surpise. She walked down her three steps.

'What!' she said, speaking into his ear. 'Didn't you know? They're going to have to close down and move this week. It's Lheureux that's making them do it, he's got them so deep into debt!' And Madame Lefrançois began to tell Monsieur Homais how the draper had lent the owners of the Café de France more money than they could ever pay back, and now they were having to sell everything.

'Look!' she said. 'There he is, Lheureux – over there, in the market. Look! He's bowing to Madame Bovary. Do look! She's got a green hat on. Do you see her? She's leaning on Monsieur Boulanger's arm.'

'Madame Bovary!' said Homais. 'Oh, I must go over and say how do you do to her! She might like to have a seat on the platform.'

Rodolphe saw him coming and walked more quickly but then, as Madame Bovary was getting out of breath, he slowed down.

'I wanted to avoid that fool – you know, that chemist fellow,' he said to her with a laugh.

Emma smiled at him.

'What does that smile mean?' he wondered. 'Is she making fun of me?' And he looked at her out of the corner of his eye as they walked on more quickly.

When they reached the corner, Rodolphe, instead of going right into the square, suddenly turned down a side-path, dragging Emma with him.

'Good evening, Monsieur Lheureux,' he called out. 'See you later.'

'You did that very well!' said Emma, laughing.

'Why should I let these people bother me? And today of all days, when I have the luck to be with you . . .'

Emma blushed. He did not finish his sentence. Then he remarked on the fine weather, and said how nice it was to walk on the grass where small yellow flowers had sprung up.

'Look,' he said, 'young girls in love use these to see if they are loved. Suppose I picked one of these. What do you think it would tell me?'

'Are you in love?' she said, with a little cough.

'Ah! Who knows?' answered Rodolphe.

The market square and the fields around continued to fill up with people. The judging was now going on and the farmers, lined up one after another, were all crowding into a ring. There were the farm animals in a long, irregular line. Among the sleepy pigs and cows, bare-armed men were holding on to great male horses which pulled with all their strength in the direction of the females. These stood quite still, holding their heads down, while their young rested in their shadows.

By now, Emma and Monsieur Boulanger had come round to the field. They discussed the people they saw, how Paris was so much more interesting than a place like Yonville, and they laughed at the fashions of the farmers' wives.

'But anyway,' he said, 'when you live in the country –'

'What's the point of looking good?'

'I agree,' answered Rodolphe. 'Not one of these people knows when a coat is well cut and when it isn't.'

And they agreed that life away from town was hardly worth living.

'Which is why,' said Rodolphe, 'I am so sad at times.'

'You!' she broke in with amazement. 'I thought you had nothing to worry about!'

'Ah, yes, it seems so, but we cannot always show the world who we really are, our true selves. Whenever I look at a cemetery by moonlight, I ask myself if I wouldn't be happier lying there asleep with the rest of them.'

'But what about your friends? You don't think of them.'

'My friends? What friends? What friends have I got? Who cares about me?'

So they walked on arm in arm, ignoring the arrival of the guests of honour, Emma leaning against this strong man with such pain in his heart. As the crowd gathered to hear the speeches, Rodolphe, accompanied by Madame Bovary, went up on to the first floor of the Town Hall into the empty council meeting room. He fetched two chairs and, bringing them close up to the window, they sat down side by side.

As soon as the speeches began, people quietened down a little, and Emma leaned forward to see better.

'I'd better get a bit farther back,' said Rodolphe.

'Why?' asked Emma.

'They might see me from down below. And then I would have to give explanations for at least a fortnight, and with my reputation . . .'

'Oh, you're making yourself sound much worse than you are,' said Emma.

'No, no; it's horrible, I tell you!'

The voice of the next speaker went on like an angry insect in the hot sun.

'But,' added Rodolphe, 'the world may be right.'

'What do you mean?' she asked.

'Well,' he said, 'don't you know that there are some people who are never at peace; people who desire dreams and action, the wildest pleasures – but after passion comes regret!'

She looked at him as if he were a traveller who has journeyed through strange and far-off lands.

'We poor women, we never have such good reasons for regret,' she said.

'Ah, but to behave as badly as I have does not make you any happier!'

'But does one ever find happiness?'

'Yes, one day,' he replied.

The speaker continued to praise the farmers, their animals and their rich fields. Some listened and some began to sleep in their seats, heads falling forward in the summer heat.

'Yes,' said Rodolphe, 'you don't have to think about it; one day you meet someone, and the horizon opens up in front of you. There are no more questions. It's as if you have already met one another in your dreams.' (Here he looked at Emma.) 'There in front of you is the jewel you have been looking for; there before your eyes. Nevertheless, you dare not believe it; you cannot see clearly, it is as if you had just stepped out of the darkness into the light.'

And as he said this, Rodolphe passed his hand over his face, then he let it fall on Emma's, who took hers away. Still the speaker read on, praising those who did their duty on the land.

'Ah, there he goes again!' said Rodolphe. 'Duty, duty – always duty! I'm sick to death of the word! We must follow our hearts – that is our true duty!'

'Yes, but – but –' said Madame Bovary, 'don't you also think we must follow the laws of society?'

'Ah! But there are two laws,' he replied. 'There is the little, unimportant man-made law, always changing, made by fools like that one down there. And there is the other, which never changes and is all around us, like the countryside and the blue heavens that give us light.'

The whole square was now crowded with people. They could be seen leaning on their elbows at every window, others standing at their doors. In spite of the silence, the speaker's voice was lost in the air. It rose in broken phrases, interrupted here and there by the sound of chairs on the stones.

Rodolphe had moved nearer to Emma, and said to her in a low voice, speaking rapidly, 'Don't society's demands disgust you? The best feelings, the purest thoughts are attacked, controlled, and if at last two souls do meet, they cannot unite. They will try, they will call out to each other. But sooner or later – in six months, ten years – they will come together, they will love; they are born for each other.'

Lifting his face towards Emma, he looked closely at her. She noticed in his eyes small golden lines coming from the dark centre, she smelt the perfume on his hair, and she half closed her eyes to breathe it in. She took off her gloves, she wiped her hands, then tried to cool her face with her handkerchief. Through the sound of her blood beating in her ears, she heard the sound of the crowd and the voice of the speaker telling them to work harder, to be good citizens.

Now Rodolphe took her hand and she did not take it away. As the names of the prize winners in the show were read out below, he told her he had never loved anyone before her, and he would love her for the rest of his life. He pressed her hand, and felt its warmth and life – like a bird held for a moment, perhaps trying to escape, perhaps responding.

'Oh, thank you, thank you!' he cried. 'You do not reject me. How sweet you are! You know that I am yours.'

Suddenly the wind rose, shaking the curtains and causing the peasant women in the square to hold on to the wings of their white hats. The speaker began to speak more quickly, more enthusiastically, but neither Rodolphe nor Emma were listening. They sat and looked into each other's eyes. Their lips were dry, their bodies full of desire, and Emma no longer felt a need to resist. Down in the square the speakers continued, the prizes were given. The celebrations would be over soon.

Madame Bovary took Rodolphe's arm, and he walked with her back to her house. They said goodbye at her front door, after which he went and walked in the fields near the river.

Chapter 10   Presents for a Lover

Six weeks went by, and Rodolphe did not contact Emma. 'I must not go back too soon,' he had said to himself. 'It would be a mistake.'

The week after the show, he went off shooting. When the hunting was over he wondered if he had left it too long, but then he thought to himself, 'If she loved me from the first day, by now she will love me even more. I will let her wait.'

When he saw how pale she became when he entered the room, he knew he had made the right decision.

She was alone and it was getting dark. Rodolphe remained standing, and Emma was barely able to answer his first greeting.

'I've been busy,' he said. 'I haven't been well.'

'Nothing serious?' she asked quickly.

'Oh, well, no,' said Rodolphe, sitting down. 'I didn't want to come here again.'

'Why?'

'Can't you guess?'

He looked at her again, but with such a look of love that she lowered her eyes with a blush.

'Emma!' he began again.

'Sir!' she cried, moving back a little.

'Ah! You see perfectly well now that I was right not to return,' he said sadly, 'but I have been thinking of you; thinking and thinking till I've become almost mad. Ah, forgive me! I'll go away – far away – and you will never hear of me again. But today, somehow, it seemed that something, I don't know what, made me come to you. Who can help falling in love with someone who is so beautiful, so charming?'

It was the first time in her life Emma had heard such words. She turned towards him with tears in her eyes.

'Oh, how kind you are!' she said.

'No,' he said, 'I love you, that's all. You know I do, don't you? Tell me you know it – just one word, one little word!' And Rodolphe began to go down on his knees. But there was a noise of someone moving around in the kitchen, and he noticed that the door was not closed.

'It would be so kind of you,' he said, getting up, 'if you could let me see your house. It's such a charming place.'

Madame Bovary said she would be happy to do this, and they were just getting up when Charles came in.

'Good morning, Doctor,' said Rodolphe. 'Madame,' he continued, 'was talking to me about her health. I was saying that a little horse riding might be a good thing.'

'An excellent idea . . . You should do that, darling.'

When she replied that she had no horse, Monsieur Rodolphe offered to lend her one. She refused, and he did not insist. And that was the end of the visit.

'Why didn't you accept Monsieur Boulanger's offer? It was very good of him,' said Charles when they were alone.

She said that perhaps people would think it rather odd.

'Well, who cares about that?' said Charles. 'Health, that's the main thing. It was silly of you.'

'And how do you expect me to go riding when I haven't got the right clothes?'

'We will get you some,' he replied.

The promise of new clothes was enough to make Emma change her mind.

When Emma's riding clothes were ready, Charles wrote to Monsieur Boulanger saying that his wife could go any time, and that they were grateful for his kind offer.

Next day, Rodolphe appeared at Charles's door with two horses. He had put on a pair of new riding-boots, telling himself that she had certainly never seen anything like them before, and Emma was charmed with the way he looked.

As soon as he felt the grass under him, Emma's horse started to move more quickly, and Rodolphe came along beside her. Every now and then they exchanged a word or two. She rode with her head a little forward, her hand well up and her right arm stretched out, and she let herself follow the movements of the horse. They rode on like this for fifteen or twenty minutes until, at the top of a small hill, the horses stopped.

It was early in October, and a thin mist was spread over the land. Sometimes the sun would shine through a break in the clouds and light up the distant roofs of Yonville, with the gardens near the water, the yards, the walls and the church. Emma half closed her eyes to see her house, and never had this poor village in which she lived seemed so small.

After a moment, Rodolphe and Emma turned off and rode along the edge of the wood. She turned away her head every now and again to avoid his eyes, and saw only the trunks of the trees. Just as they entered the wood, the sun came out.

'God is with us!' said Rodolphe.

'You think so?' she answered.

'Come on! Come on!' was his reply.

The path narrowed as they went into the wood, and sometimes, to keep away the branches, he rode close up to her and Emma felt his knee rubbing against her leg. The sky was blue now, and not a leaf moved. They got down from their horses and Emma walked a little further down the path. Rodolphe came up behind her, stretched out his arm and put it round her waist. She made an effort to break away, but he continued to hold her, so she turned and walked back towards where they had stopped.

'Oh, stay!' said Rodolphe. 'We must not go yet! Stay!'

And he took her to a little pool, whose surface was covered with small green water plants.

'It is wrong of me! Wrong, wrong!' she cried. 'I am mad to listen to you.'

'Why? Emma! Emma!'

'Oh, Rodolphe!' she cried, dropping her head against his shoulder.

With a deep sigh she threw back her head, giving her white neck to his kisses and, almost fainting, in tears, her whole body shaking with emotion, hiding her face in her hands, she surrendered herself to him.

When evening began to fall the sun, shining through the branches, was bright in her eyes. Everywhere was silence. She could feel her heart as it began to beat again, she could feel the blood moving through her body like a stream of milk. And then, far, far away, beyond the wood, on the hills across the valley, she heard a cry, strange and distant, a voice that hung in the air, and she listened to it in silence. Rodolphe was standing with a cigar between his teeth, cleaning his fingernails with a small knife.

They returned to Yonville by the way they had come. They saw the tracks of their horses in the soil, side by side, and there were the same bushes and the same stones in the grass. Nothing about them had changed, but for her something had happened, something more surprising than if the mountains had fallen into the sea.

When she was alone in her room after dinner, she looked at herself in the mirror and was amazed at her own face. Never had her eyes looked so big, so dark, so deep. It was as if she had become another woman. And she kept saying to herself over and over again, 'I have a lover, a lover.'

From that first day they wrote to each other every night. Emma took her letter to the end of the garden near the river and put it in a gap in the wall. Rodolphe would come and take it and put another in its place, and always she complained that his letters were too short.

The time she had with him was too short too, so whenever Charles was called out early, Emma got up, threw on some clothes and ran through the fields to Rodolphe's house. At this early hour Rodolphe would still be asleep, and Emma seemed like a spring morning coming into his room. Laughing, he would pull her towards him and down on to his breast, and afterwards it would take them a quarter of an hour to say goodbye. Emma would burst out crying; she would have liked to stay with Rodolphe always and never leave him any more. But one day, when she came in unexpectedly, a look of annoyance passed over his face.

'What's the matter?' she said. 'Don't you feel well? Tell me!'

At first he said nothing, but then, looking very serious about it, he told her that he was worried about these early morning visits. People would start talking about her. They needed another meeting place.

Rodolphe said he would look out for a house outside Yonville where they could be together, but all through the winter, three or four times a week, and when it was quite dark, the only place they could find was Emma's garden. They would come together there after Charles had gone to sleep. The cold made them hold each other tighter; their eyes, though they could hardly see them in the growing darkness, seemed bigger. On wet nights they would take shelter in the surgery. She would light one of the kitchen candles and Rodolphe made himself quite at home. The sight of the bookcase and the desk – everything in the room, in fact – seemed to amuse him, and he could not stop himself from making all sorts of little jokes about Charles. This did not please Emma. She would have liked him to be a little more serious, a little more dramatic.

But Rodolphe felt no need to change his ways and was, in fact, becoming a little bored with Emma's delicate emotions and sensitivities. She even talked about wanting a ring – a proper wedding ring – as a symbol of their union. He never spoke to her now as he used to, saying the sweet, tender things that had made her cry with happiness. He never kissed her and held her in the old way. No! That great love of theirs, on whose waves she had been carried away, seemed to be growing shallower beneath her, like the waters of a river in a dry summer, and now she could see the mud that lay beneath it!

As Emma grew to understand that this great love affair might not be for ever, Rodolphe found her becoming more and more distant, even cooler towards him. For a few weeks she even spent more time with Charles, trying to see if she could love him better. But it was no use, and Rodolphe thought to himself, 'She'll get over it. It's just one of her little ways.'

He was right. All he had to do was to keep away, to miss their meeting for three or four nights, and once again her complaints stopped and she was his!

So love began for them again. Often, in the middle of the day, Emma would take up a pen and write to him. And she did not only send letters, but also presents, small expensive things that she could not afford, and which she could not ask her husband to buy.

It was Monsieur Lheureux, the draper, who was able to help her here. As soon as he heard that Madame Bovary was buying gifts for someone, he made sure he met her as often as he could. He told her all about the latest deliveries from Paris, was very helpful and never asked for his money. Emma found this a very easy way to satisfy her wish to please her lover, and she took full advantage of it. For example, she wanted to buy Rodolphe a very handsome riding whip that was on show at an umbrella shop in Rouen. And next week, there was Monsieur Lheureux putting it on her dining room table.

But the day after that, he came along with a bill for two hundred and seventy francs! Emma did not know what to do. All the drawers in the desk had been emptied out. She owed wages to the servants, and Bovary was anxiously waiting for a payment from Monsieur Derozerays, who, in previous years, had always paid his doctor's bill some time in July.

At first she managed to get rid of Lheureux, but in the end he lost patience. He had to pay his bills, other people were asking him for the money! He would be forced to ask her to return the goods.

'Very well, take them,' said Emma.

'Oh, I was only joking!' he replied. 'The only thing that worries me is the riding whip. I know! I'll ask the doctor to let me have it back.'

'No, don't!' she cried out.

'Aha, I've got you!' thought Lheureux to himself. And, sure of being on the right track, he went out, saying under his breath, 'Right! We shall see, we shall see!'

She was wondering how she was going to get out of this difficulty when the maid came in and put a little packet on the table, 'From Monsieur Derozerays.' Emma took the envelope and tore it open. It was enough money to pay her debts! She heard Charles coming up the stairs and, without thinking, she threw the money to the back of the drawer, locked it, and took out the key.

Three days later Lheureux reappeared.

'I want to suggest an arrangement,' he said. 'If, instead of the sum agreed, you would . . .'

'There you are,' said she, putting the four hundred francs in his hand. She was safe for the moment, but what would happen next time? What could she do to escape?

Her dream now was to go away with Rodolphe. One night when they met in the garden, and she was at her saddest and most beautiful, he asked her what he could do to help her, to bring back the smile to her face.

'What must we do? What do you want?'

'Take me away!' she cried. 'Take me from here . . . Oh, I beg you!'

'But . . .' Rodolphe began.

'Yes?'

'What about your little girl?'

She thought a minute or two and then answered, 'We'll take her with us. It's the only thing to do.'

'What a woman!' he said to himself, as he saw her disappear. Someone was calling.

But now Emma believed that she would be able to escape, and this became her only topic of conversation with Rodolphe. She would lean her head on his shoulder and whisper, 'Ah, when we are in the coach! Can you imagine it? Is it possible? It seems to me that the moment I feel it moving, it will be as if we were going up in a balloon, as if we were going to the clouds. Do you know, I'm counting the days! Aren't you?'

Never had Madame Bovary looked so beautiful as now. Charles thought her as delicious as on the day she became his bride. When he came home late at night, he did not dare to wake her. The night-lamp threw a ring of light on the ceiling as she lay sleeping beside her daughter. Charles would stand and look at them, dreaming of the future, of his beautiful wife and his growing child. But he was not in Emma's dreams; she was heading for a new land in a coach pulled by four white horses and with her lover by her side.

She was so certain she would be leaving that she sent for Monsieur Lheureux and ordered a heavy travelling coat and a travelling case. She told him to keep the things at the shop when they arrived, and she would collect them in a week or two. It was, in fact, the following month that they were going to run away. She would leave Yonville as if she were going shopping in Rouen. Rodolphe would have booked the seats, arranged the passports, and written to Paris in order to have the mail coach all to themselves as far as Marseilles. There they would buy a carriage and go right through to Genoa. In all this planning the child was never mentioned, and Rodolphe avoided any reference to her; perhaps Emma had given up the idea of taking her.

However, Rodolphe then found he needed a fortnight to complete certain business matters; then, after a week, he needed another fortnight. Then he found he was not feeling very well so there was another delay, and then he went away on a journey. The whole of August went by and finally, after all these delays, the date of their departure was fixed for 4 September, a Monday.

On the evening of their last Saturday in Yonville, Rodolphe came to see her earlier than usual.

'Is everything ready?' she asked.

'Yes.'

'You're sad,' said Emma.

'No. Why?'

'Is it because you are going away?' she went on. 'Leaving the things you love, the things that have been your life? Ah, I understand! But I, I have nothing in the world! You are everything to me. And so I shall be everything to you.'

'Oh, what a lovely night!' said Rodolphe.

'We shall have many more nights together,' she answered. And then, as if speaking to herself, she went on, 'Yes, it will be good to travel. But why is my heart so sad? Is it fear of the unknown . . . or the break with all I have been used to? Or else . . . ? No, it is because I am too happy in my happiness! How weak I am! Forgive me!'

'There is still time,' he exclaimed. 'Think! You may regret it later.'

'Never!' she cried.

The clock struck twelve.

'Midnight!' she said. 'Tomorrow is already here! We have just one more day to wait!'

He rose to go.

'You've got the passports?'

'Yes.'

'You haven't forgotten anything?'

'No.'

'You're sure?'

'Quite sure.'

'You'll be waiting for me at the Hôtel de Provence, won't you? At twelve o'clock?'

He nodded.

'Tomorrow, then!' said Emma, and she watched him go.

He did not look back.

After a few minutes Rodolphe stopped, and when he saw her white figure disappear into the shadows his heart began to beat so wildly that he had to lean against a tree to keep himself from falling.

'What a fool I am! But, never mind, she was a fine little woman!' And as he said it, Emma's beauty, the thought of all the times they had had together, came back into his mind. For a moment tears came to his eyes, but then he felt a wave of anger against her. 'After all,' he cried, 'I couldn't just go and bury myself alive like that – and have to look after the child too! And think of the worry, the expense! Ah, no, it would have been too silly!'

Chapter 11 Goodbye

The letter Rodolphe wrote that evening ended with the words:

> . . . I shall be far away when you read these sad lines. I have made
> up my mind to go at once, so that I cannot see you again! I shall
> come back, no doubt, and perhaps one day we shall talk together
> of the time when we were lovers.
> Your Friend.

As she read these words the next morning, Emma's first thought was to kill herself. Life no longer had meaning; how could she eat another meal, sit in the same room as her husband? Rodolphe! How could she live without him? The room started to spin around her, nothing was still, she could not see, and everything went black.

Then Charles was shouting for help, Berthe was screaming, and Félicité, the maid, with shaking hands, was loosening her mistress's clothing. Emma herself lay stretched out on the floor, shaking from head to foot.

'Speak! speak!' Charles kept on saying. 'Emma! It's me, your own Charles, who loves you. Don't you know me? Here! Here's your little one. Kiss her, Emma!'

The child stretched out her arms to her mother, to put them round her neck. But Emma turned away her head and cried, 'No, no . . . No one!'

She fainted away again. They carried her up to bed. She lay there, her mouth open, her eyes shut, her hands open, quite still. The tears ran from her eyes on to the pillow.

For forty-three days Charles never left Emma's side. His patients had to take care of themselves. He called in Monsieur Canivet, in consultation. He sent to Rouen for Dr Larivière, his old master; he was desperate. What scared him most was Emma's depressed condition. She did not speak, took no notice of anything, and did not even seem to suffer – as if her soul and body were both resting after the shock through which they had passed.

About halfway through October she was able to sit up in bed, supported by pillows. Charles cried when he saw her eating her first piece of bread and jam. She began to recover her strength and got up for an hour or two in the afternoons, and one day, when she was feeling much better, he persuaded her to walk a little in the garden, leaning on his arm. So they went, arm in arm, to the bottom of the garden and its low wall. Slowly she looked up and, shading her eyes with her hand, she looked away, far, far away, into the distance. But there was nothing on the skyline except the smoke of burning grass on the hills.

She turned back to look into the garden, and remembered Rodolphe, remembered their nights of love in this place, and fell back into Charles's arms, seeing nothing. That night she was as ill as before, though this time her condition was more complicated. First it was her heart that troubled her. Then her chest, or her head. Then she had attacks of vomiting, which Charles thought might be the early signs of cancer. And on top of all this trouble, the poor man was worried about money.

First, he did not know how he was going to pay Monsieur Homais for all the medicines he had had from him. And the bills kept pouring in. Monsieur Lheureux, the draper, was especially difficult. In fact, when Emma's illness was at its worst, Lheureux, taking advantage of the situation, had rushed over with the coat, the travelling bag, two travelling boxes instead of one, and other unordered items as well! Charles, of course, said he had no use for them, but it was no good; the goods had been ordered, and the draper was not going to take them back. In the end, Bovary found himself signing a document promising to pay in six months – and then borrowing another thousand francs! So Charles's problems worsened, while Lheureux was delighted to have both husband and wife in his debt. He saw it as a good investment.

Charles often wondered how he was going to pay all this money back next year. He thought and thought; maybe he should ask his father for help, or sell something. But his father would not listen, and he – well, he had nothing to sell. And then the whole situation began to look so black that he hurriedly pushed it out of his mind.

The winter was a hard one, and Emma took longer to recover this time. When the weather was fine, they pushed her chair up to the window, so that she could look out on the square. She had now taken a violent dislike to the garden, and the curtains on that side were always closed. Now she passed her time reading religious texts which the priest brought for her, and Rodolphe was pushed back into a hidden place in her heart. And although her recovery continued, she was so much changed that she even enjoyed the company of the respectable married women of Yonville.

When the spring came, she had the whole garden torn up from end to end. Her old energy had begun to return as her health improved, and although Monsieur Bournisien, the priest, still continued to visit her every day, she went to church less often. She began to enjoy time spent out of doors, looking over the new garden, even sitting outside with Charles and Monsieur Homais in the warmer evenings. It was on one of these evenings, as Monsieur Homais talked about the pleasures one could gain from literature and music, that the idea of going to see *Lucia di Lammermoor** at the theatre in Rouen was raised. Emma was against the idea at first, but Charles felt that the change would do her good, and he wanted to give her a little pleasure, despite his debts and their other worries. So Monsieur and Madame Bovary drove in to Rouen on the Friday coach and got down at the Hôtel de la Croix Rouge, in the place† Beauvoisine. Leaving Emma at the hotel, Charles at once went out to buy tickets for the theatre.

Chapter 12   A Visit to the Theatre

Emma was pleased that her husband had bought good seats, and when she sat down she could not resist a little smile of pride as she looked at the ordinary people down below. Soon the candles

---

* *Lucia di Lammermoor*: an opera by Donizetti (1797–1848) based on Sir Walter Scott's story of a young woman who fights for her freedom to choose her own lover, but who goes mad and dies in the end.

† place: the French word for a town square.

were being lit, the musicians were taking their places and the opera was starting. When they began to play, she lost herself in the music, her eyes almost blinded by the richness of the colours, the beauty of the singers. And their voices, their beautiful bodies dressed in the finest clothes you could imagine, their noble emotions – it was too much!

Poor Charles, however, could understand none of it.

'Why is he so unkind to her?' he whispered.

'But he isn't,' she answered. 'He's her lover.'

Emma tried to explain as well as she could, but he confessed that he could not follow the story because all this music stopped him from hearing the words.

'What does it matter?' said Emma. 'Be quiet!'

'Well, you see,' he answered, leaning over on her shoulder, 'I like to understand things; you know I always do.'

'Oh, please be quiet!' she cried impatiently.

So Charles sat in silence while Emma became more and more involved in the story of the tragic heroine, a story which made her think about her own life. As the singer came to the front of the stage, supported by her women, white flowers in her hair, and as pale as death, Emma began dreaming of her own marriage. She saw herself back again on the little footpath, when she and her father were making their way to the church. Why had she not fought against her father, as Lucia had done? Instead, she had been happy and light-hearted, never realizing how she was throwing herself away!

The curtain fell at the end of the first act. Emma wanted to go out; the corridors were crowded with people, and she sank back in her seat feeling as if she could not breathe. Charles thought she was going to faint, and rushed off to the bar to get her a glass of water. When he returned with the water, he also brought the news that he had seen Monsieur Léon.

'Léon?'

'The man himself! He's coming round in a minute to see you!'

And before these words were out of his mouth, the ex-clerk from Yonville came and sat beside her. He put out his hand, and Madame Bovary gave him hers, mechanically, as if obeying some force of attraction she could not resist. She had not felt this hand since that spring evening when the rain was falling on the green leaves and they said goodbye standing beside the window.

'Oh, how do you do? Imagine it! You here?'

They could not talk now, as the opera had begun again, but from that moment she stopped listening. Everything seemed to be taking place far away, like the sound of music from a distant room.

As soon as the opera had finished, all three of them went and sat in the open air, outside a café. They began by talking about her illness, Emma interrupting Charles every now and then for fear, she said, of boring Monsieur Léon. Then Léon told them how he was going to spend two years in a lawyer's office here in Rouen. He said that he needed the experience as the work in Normandy was very different from the kind of thing he had been doing in Paris.

People coming away from the theatre passed along in front of them on the pavement, some still singing the tunes from the opera. Although Léon had not been impressed by the leading male singer, Charles (who had begun to understand things better towards the end of the show) had appreciated his voice and said he would love to hear him again.

'Oh, well,' said Léon, 'he'll be giving another performance soon.'

But Charles replied that they were going home in the morning. 'Unless you'd like to stay a little longer by yourself,' he added, turning to his wife.

When Léon saw that there was a chance Emma might be able to stay, he began to praise the singer, and Charles became even more certain that she must stay in Rouen for an extra night.

'You can come back on Sunday. It's silly of you not to stay, if you feel it's doing you even the slightest bit of good.'

And so it was arranged that Charles would return to Yonville in the morning, and Léon would go to the opera with Madame Bovary on the following evening.

Since leaving Yonville, Léon had not forgotten Emma. In Paris, he had worked at his studies and had not had the wild time he had imagined. It had been a happy but unexciting period, and he had sometimes dreamed of the love that might have been between them. Seeing her again, after three long years, all his hopes returned. This time he thought he really would have to bring things to a conclusion. He was less shy now, more sure of himself, and after his time in Paris he felt quite confident that he could have his way with this country doctor's wife. He would not have been brave enough to make the attempt in Paris, but away from the capital he had the courage.

When they met the following afternoon, he did his best to make himself interesting to her. He talked, therefore, about how unhappy he had been since he left Yonville, and how his dreams had been disappointed.

'If you only knew,' she said, 'the dreams that I have dreamed.' And tears shone in her beautiful eyes as she raised them to the ceiling.

'And I, too!' cried Léon. 'I often went out, trying to lose myself in the noise of the crowd, but I was never able to get you out of my thoughts.'

Madame Bovary turned away her head so that he should not see the smile she felt on her lips. She let him speak, saying nothing, waiting for him to say what she wanted to hear. She did not have to wait long.

'And,' he went on, 'I wrote you so many letters that I never sent.'

'But why?' she asked.

'Why?' And he hesitated a moment. 'Because I loved you!'

Congratulating himself for having said the words, Léon watched her out of the corner of his eye.

It was like looking at the sky after the sun has chased away the clouds. Her whole face was lit up with joy.

He waited, and at last she said, 'I always thought you did.'

Then they talked about all the things that had happened when he lived in Yonville. They spoke of the flowers in her garden, the dresses she used to wear, the furniture in her bedroom, and of all the things in and around the house. They talked and talked, and before they realized how time had passed, it was eight o'clock.

She rose to light the candles; then she came and sat down again.

'Well?' said Léon, and he reached out and touched her hand. 'What could stop us from beginning all over again now?'

'No, my friend,' she replied. 'I am too old . . . you are too young . . . Forget all about me. Others will love you . . . and you will love them.'

'Not as I love you,' he cried.

'What a child you are! We have to be sensible! I mean it!'

And she did mean it – she intended to keep her distance, to be responsible. She had suffered too much to want to open those wounds again. However, she was not prepared for Léon's shyness. If he had been another Rodolphe, it would have been easy; she could have pushed him away without an effort. But Léon was so beautiful, so full of desire for her – she could see it in his eyes – but so gentle, she did not know what to do. When he took her face in his hands and kissed her, she could not resist, because he did it without force, with such care. But still, she could not let this happen!

So she looked at the clock above the fireplace and said,

'Heavens, look at the time! We have forgotten all about the theatre! And I must go back to my poor husband tomorrow, so there is my last chance gone!'

'Are you really going back?' said Léon.

'I am.'

'But I must see you again,' he said. 'I had something I wanted to tell you . . .'

'What is it?'

'Something . . . Oh, something very serious, very important! Ah, but no! You won't go back. You can't. If you only knew . . . Listen, you mustn't go like this! Let me see you again, I beg you. Once, just once!'

'Well . . .' And she stopped. And then, as if on second thoughts, she said, 'Oh, no. Not here!'

'Wherever you like.'

'Will you . . . ?' She seemed to be thinking. Then suddenly she said, 'Tomorrow, at eleven, in the cathedral.'

'I shall be there,' he cried, taking both her hands.

But that night Emma wrote a long, long letter, excusing herself from meeting him. It was all over now, and, for their own sakes, it would be better for them not to meet. But when the letter was sealed up, she realized she did not know Léon's address.

'I will give it to him myself,' she said. 'He is sure to come.'

Léon arrived early at the cathedral, and had to wait in the cool shadows for what seemed like hours. Suddenly, at around eleven o'clock, there was the sound of silk upon the stones, the shadow of a hat on the wall . . . It was Emma! Léon rose and went to meet her.

Emma was pale, and she was walking quickly.

'Read this!' she said, holding out a paper. But then, seeming to change her mind, she cried out, 'Oh no! Never mind!'

And she quickly tore away her hand, and went out into the

sunshine again. She did not know what to do, how to go on. She wanted to be here, to be with him, and at the same time to fly, fly away.

Léon followed, feeling that his love was in danger of disappearing like smoke. Wanting to take back control of the situation (which he felt was slipping through his fingers), he decided to hire one of the carriages which were waiting. They could drive away, be together in this private, dark space. They could not go to his room, nor to hers, so a carriage, hired for the day, would be their shelter.

'Léon, really . . . I don't know whether I ought. It's not the proper thing to do. You know it isn't!'

'Why not?' answered the clerk. 'It's done in Paris.'

Emma had no reply to this.

'Where to, sir?' said the driver.

'Wherever you like,' said Léon, pushing Emma inside; and so they set off, first going down to the bridge over the river, then across the main square, past the town hall and stopping beside a statue.

'Keep going,' said a voice from inside.

The carriage started again and, following the downhill road after leaving the centre of town, it drove at full speed into the square in front of the railway station.

'No, no, straight on!' shouted the voice again.

The driver took them out of town through the big gates, down to the waterside. Along by the river the vehicle went, towards the little town of Oyssel.

And on and on went the carriage, with its sweating driver and tired horse. Each time they stopped, the man's voice cried out, 'Drive on, drive on!' until, at about six in the evening, the carriage stopped in a side street and a woman got out. She walked away with her face hidden, looking neither to the right nor to the left.

Chapter 13   Love Once More

When she got back to her hotel, Emma was shocked not to find the Yonville coach. The driver had waited fifty-three minutes, and had at last set off without her. Although there was no strong reason why she should go home, she had promised that she would be back that evening, and she knew Charles would be expecting her. In her heart she was also feeling guilty for her afternoon of love with Léon. Going home this evening was an easy way of making herself feel better about what she had just done. So she threw her things into her bag, paid her bill, hired a small carriage from the hotel and, telling the driver to drive like the wind, managed to catch up with the coach just as it was driving into Quincampoix.

She had hardly sunk into her corner when she closed her eyes, and did not open them again till they were at the bottom of the hill. Some way off, she recognized her maid, Félicité, who was waiting for her at the entrance to the village.

The driver pulled in to the side, and the maid called up to her mistress, 'Madame, you must go at once to Monsieur Homais. Something very urgent!'

The village was as quiet as usual, but when she went into Monsieur Homais' house she found the pharmacist waiting for her with a serious expression on his face.

'Madame, I fear I have bad news for you. Your father-in-law is dead!'

In fact, Monsieur Bovary senior had died the previous evening quite suddenly just after getting up from dinner. As Charles was anxious that Emma should not be upset, he had asked Monsieur Homais to break the news to her. He had thought it might be less of a shock if it came from someone outside the family. Although Charles's thought was kind, Emma was not, in fact, greatly upset, and went immediately to her house.

When he heard Emma knock, Charles came forward to greet her with open arms and said, with tears in his voice, 'Ah! My dear...'

He bent down to kiss her, but at the touch of his lips, the memory of her lover took hold of her and she passed her hand over her face to hide her look of disgust. Nevertheless, she managed to say, 'Yes, I know... I know ...'

He showed her the letter in which his mother told him the news. Emma gave the letter back, and at dinner, out of politeness, pretended to have no appetite. But as he encouraged her, she forced herself to eat, while Charles sat facing her in motionless sorrow. Every now and then he would raise his head and look at her sadly. Once he said, 'I wish I could have seen him one more time!' She made no answer. Then, realizing that some sort of comment was required of her, she asked, 'How old was your father?'

'Fifty-eight.'

'Oh!'

And that was all.

A quarter of an hour afterwards he added, 'Poor mother! What will happen to her now?'

Emma had no idea, and made a silent gesture.

Feeling that her silence was the result of sorrow at the news, Charles made an effort to be more cheerful.

'Did you have a good time yesterday?'

'Yes,' she replied.

When the table was cleared, neither Bovary nor Emma moved. As she continued to look at him, she found that she could not pity him. He seemed a weak thing, a poor man in every way. How could she get rid of him? The evening would be endless!

Next day Charles's mother arrived, and the weeping started again. Emma said she had a lot of things to organize and went out. Charles thought of his father, and he was surprised at feeling so affectionate towards him. He had never thought he loved his father. Madame Bovary senior also thought of her husband. It was all over now, and even the worst of her days with him were pleasant memories.

While the son thought about his lost father, Emma thought that only forty-eight hours earlier she and Léon were together, with the world shut out, drowning in love, amazed by each other's beauty. She tried to recover the details of that lost day of happiness and pleasure. She would have liked to hear and see nothing new in order not to lose a moment of remembered delight, but she found that her husband's noisy sorrow was driving it all from her memory.

The next afternoon, when all three of them were sitting in the garden, they saw Monsieur Lheureux coming through the gate. He had heard of the sad event, and had come to visit them. After he had expressed his sorrow at their loss, he said to Charles, 'Could I have a word in private with your wife? It's about that matter, er . . . you know!'

Charles blushed to the roots of his hair as he answered, 'Ah, yes . . . of course. Darling, do you think . . . ?'

She seemed to understand, and got up.

'It's nothing!' said Charles to his mother. 'Only a little household matter.'

As soon as they were alone, Monsieur Lheureux began to congratulate Emma on the money she and her husband would have now that Monsieur Bovary's father had died.

'And as you are well again,' he continued, 'I was coming to make proposals for another arrangement.'

What he in fact proposed was that Emma should take over the responsibility for all the debts 'to stop her husband worrying'. Then she and Monsieur Lheureux would be able to settle all the details.

She did not understand, so she said nothing. Lheureux quickly added that there were some things that Madame could not possibly do without. For example, he would send her across a dozen metres of beautiful black silk for a dress.

'The one you have on is good enough for the house, but you need another one for visiting. I saw that straight away, when I came in.'

He did not send the fabric; he brought it. Then he came back for the measurements. He kept coming back, doing everything he could to be of use, to make himself liked. And every time he came, he reminded her that she should be the one who managed the couple's legal and financial affairs. He never mentioned the old bills, and she never let them enter her head. Charles certainly had said something about them when she was beginning to get better, but she had so many things to worry her at the time that she thought no more about them.

Moreover, she avoided starting any discussion about money while her mother-in-law was there. But, as soon as she had left, Emma began to amaze her husband with her practical good sense. They really did have to manage things better. She used a number of technical terms, spoke impressively about planning for the future, and never missed a chance of exaggerating how complicated it would be to make the right arrangements. Finally, she put in front of him one day a form which gave her the power to manage all his financial affairs. She had profited well from Lheureux's lessons.

Charles – good, simple man – asked her where the form came from. She told him it had been written by Monsieur Guillaumin, the Yonville lawyer, and then added, 'But I wouldn't trust him further than I could see him. These lawyers are nearly as bad as the criminals they work with. Perhaps we ought to consult . . . No, there's no one!'

'What about Léon?' said Charles, thinking hard.

74

He had said exactly the name Emma wanted him to say. Now she could suggest that it was difficult to explain matters by letter, and she offered to go over to Rouen and speak to him directly. Charles would not hear of troubling her. She insisted. It was a battle of kindness. Finally, she cried, 'Now, not another word, please! I am going!'

'How kind you are!' he said, kissing her on the forehead.

The next morning she was off to Rouen in the coach, to consult Monsieur Léon. She stayed for three days.

They were three wonderful days. They stayed down near the harbour at the Hôtel de Boulogne, and there they lived, with the curtains closed, the doors locked, the floor covered with flowers, and iced drinks brought up every morning. Towards evening they would take a boat and go and have dinner on one of the islands. As they left the town, smoke rose up among the trees, and the red sun, reflected on the oily water of the harbour, looked like blood on polished metal. They went down between the rows of boats, and the noises of the town grew fainter and fainter. When, finally, they arrived at their favourite restaurant, she untied her hat and they stepped out of the boat on to their island.

They went into a small café with dark fishing-nets hung up at the door, and sat themselves down in the low-ceilinged room. They ate small fried fish, followed by cherries and cream, and then went and sat on the grass. They kissed and held one another under the trees, out of view; they would have liked to live for ever in that little spot which, in their present happiness, they thought the most beautiful place on earth. They had both seen trees before, and blue sky, and grass. It was not the first time they had heard the sound of water and the music of the wind in the trees, but they had never really admired these things till now. It was as if nature had not really existed before, or had only begun to show its beauty after they had satisfied their desires.

When it was dark, they started for home again. The boat kept close to the shores of the little islands. They did not speak, but sat silently in the back of the boat, listening to the water. Emma looked across at Léon. Her head was raised, her hands were held together, her eyes raised to the sky. She was beautiful tonight. Then Léon put his hand on a piece of red ribbon lying in the bottom of the boat. The boatman took it and examined it.

'Ah,' he said at last, 'maybe it belongs to one of the people I took out a few days ago. They were having fun I can tell you – ladies and gentlemen, with cakes, and bottles of wine. I remember one of them in particular. A fine, handsome man he was, with a little moustache. Lord, he was funny, though! They kept on saying, "Come on, tell us another... Adolphe... Rodolphe..." Yes, Rodolphe, that was his name.'

Emma shook from head to foot.

'What's the matter?' said Léon, moving closer.

'Oh, it's nothing! The night air is a little cool.'

'The sort of gentleman who has plenty of lady friends,' added the old boatman.

The morning after this last dinner on the island, Emma had to return to Yonville, and Léon had to get back to his normal life in Rouen. However, he found this difficult and he started ignoring his friends and not looking after his business. Every day he waited for her letters; he read them again and again, and he wrote back to her immediately, remembering every detail of their time together. And unlike most memories, these did not seem to fade, but grew stronger. The need to see her became so great that one Saturday morning he ran out of his office and took the coach to Yonville.

When he came to the top of the hill above the village and, looking down over the valley, saw the church tower, he felt like a man who has gone abroad and made his fortune and now returns to visit his native village. He walked down to her house and saw that there was a light in the kitchen. He watched to see if he could catch sight of her shadow behind the curtain. But nothing could be seen.

Madame Lefrançois met him, and could not believe her eyes. He had dinner in the little dining room, as in the old days, but alone. He then went and knocked at the doctor's door. Madame was upstairs in her bedroom, and did not come down for a quarter of an hour. The doctor appeared delighted to see him and, to their regret, stayed at home all that day and the next. The only chance to see her alone came very late in the evening, in the lane at the end of the garden – the lane where she used to meet 'the other one'. There was a thunderstorm and they talked under an umbrella, with lightning flashing all around them.

Their separation was becoming impossible to bear. 'I would rather be dead,' she said, holding him, with tears in her eyes.

'Goodbye! Goodbye! When shall I see you again?'

They turned back for one last kiss, and she promised to find some way of seeing him regularly, at least once a week. She was full of hope. She would soon have some money to play with.

In fact, she was soon behaving as if she had all the money in the world. She bought a pair of yellow curtains for her bedroom, which Monsieur Lheureux had told her were a bargain. She had dreams of a carpet and Lheureux, saying that to want a carpet was not like wishing for the moon, helped her to get one. She had begun to depend on Lheureux. She sent for him twenty times a day, and he immediately stopped what he was doing and came to see Madame. It was a dangerous friendship for Emma.

It was about this time – around the beginning of winter – that she suddenly appeared to develop a tremendous enthusiasm for music. One night, while Charles was listening to her, she began the same piece over again, stopping four times, finding fault with herself each time. He, never noticing any difference, cried, 'Oh well done! Splendid! What did you stop for? Go on!'

'Oh, no! It's too bad! My fingers feel as if they were stiff with rust!'

Next day he begged her to play him something more.

'Oh, well, if you want me to.'

Charles confessed he had heard her play better. She kept hitting the wrong notes, and finally came to a sudden stop.

'Ah, it's no good! I ought to have some lessons, but . . .' She bit her lip and added, 'Twenty francs a time. It's too expensive!'

'Well, yes . . . it is . . .' said Charles. 'But perhaps it could be managed a bit cheaper. Sometimes a less well-known artist can be better than a teacher with a big reputation.'

'They are not easy to find,' said Emma, and did not open the piano again – although whenever she went near it (if Charles was in the room) she would say sadly, 'Ah, my poor piano!'

And when she had visitors, she never failed to tell them she had given up her music and could not now start again because of their lack of money. And they would say what a pity it was, since she had such a gift. They even spoke to Charles about it, especially the pharmacist, saying it was really too bad of him.

'You're making a mistake. You should never let a natural gift lie unused. Besides, my friend, you should remember that by encouraging your wife to study now, you will be saving on your child's musical education later. In my opinion, children ought always to be taught by their own mother.'

So Charles again came back to this piano question. Emma replied bitterly that they might as well sell it, for all the good it was. But to sell this piano, something she had been so proud of, was an idea that Bovary could not accept.

'Well,' he said, 'if you want a lesson now and again, it might be possible.'

'Yes,' she replied, 'but it's no good having lessons unless you take them regularly.'

That was how she managed to get permission from her

husband to go to Rouen once a week to see her lover. At the end of a month, everyone said that she had made a lot of progress.

Chapter 14   Debts

Thursday was the day. She got up and dressed very quietly, in order not to disturb Charles, and took the early coach to Rouen, arriving just as the city was beginning to wake up. For fear of being seen, she usually avoided the main streets, going instead down narrow lanes and alleys until she reached the rue★ Nationale, and turned down a side street, and yes, there he was.

Léon made no sign, but continued on his way. She followed him until they came to the hotel. In he went and up the stairs, opened the door of their room and entered; and then how they kissed, and then how they talked! They spoke of all the worries they had had during the week, all the things they had done. But that was all over now, and they looked at each other with little sounds of delight, and words of tenderness and love.

The bed was large, with red curtains, and there was nothing so beautiful in the world as her dark head and white skin against the dark red when, with a shy little gesture, she put her arms together and hid her face in her hands. How they loved this room. They had their lunch by the fire on a little side-table. They were so completely involved in each other that it seemed like being in their own home, and they dreamed they would continue to live there always. They talked about 'our room', and for the first time in his life Léon tasted the sweetness of female company, a woman's life.

He knelt on the ground in front of her and, with his two elbows on her knees, looked at her with a smile, leaning his face

★ rue: the French word for street.

79

towards her. And she leaned down to him, and whispered, 'Oh, don't move! Don't speak! Look at me! There is something in your eyes so sweet – it does me so much good.' And she called him 'child': 'Do you love me, child?' And she hardly heard his reply, so wildly did he press his lips to her mouth.

At the end of their day she would say, 'Goodbye till Thursday! Thursday!'

Then suddenly she would seize his head in both her hands, kiss him quickly on the forehead and, crying 'Goodbye', run down the stairs.

Charles would be at home and waiting for her and, at last, Madame arrived. She hardly looked at her child and, if dinner was late, did not criticize the cook. Often her husband, seeing how pale she was, asked her if she was feeling ill.

'No,' said Emma.

'But,' he answered, 'you seem so strange tonight.'

'Oh, no! It's nothing. I'm all right.'

But her whole life had become a lie, in which her love for Léon lay hidden from the world. Lying became a necessary part of her day, almost a hobby.

One day, however, Monsieur Lheureux met her in Rouen as she was coming out of the Hôtel de Boulogne with Léon; it gave her a shock, and she thought he would tell everyone. He was not such a fool. But three days later he came into her room, shut the door behind him and said, 'I need some money, and soon.'

She told him she could not let him have any. Lheureux reminded her how helpful he had always been and pulled out of his pocket an account of goods not paid for – more than two thousand francs.

She lowered her head.

'But if you haven't got cash, you've got property,' and he mentioned a farm near Aumale that Charles had inherited from his father. Lheureux knew everything — how big the farm was, how much rent it was worth.

'If I were you,' he said, 'I would pay my debts, and there would still be some money left over.'

He came back the following week, saying that after a lot of trouble he had found a buyer willing to pay four thousand francs for the farm. Emma was happier than she had been for months. But Lheureux shook his head and told her how much richer she would be if she let him manage these affairs. Finally he persuaded her to borrow even more money from him and to sign a series of documents which she did not understand. He told her this would give her more cash now — cash she could use to pay her other debts and buy some of the little things she wanted. Emma, with her mind full of thoughts of Léon and what they could do together, did not even read the papers, but simply signed her name where Lheureux placed his dirty finger. With this money in her hands, she felt she might begin to be free.

Freedom, however, was a disappointment. Despite her hopes, she now found Léon less pleased to meet her than before, less in love. Because she had more money in her pocket she made more demands on him, but his employer was worried about his work, and his friends asked him why they could no longer see him. And the more Emma demanded, the less Léon wanted to give, and while her love, her need continued to grow, so did her anger. In the end, she brought roses for him from Yonville and threw them in his face.

So Emma was not happy. Why was there this emptiness in her life? Why did whatever she want turn into dust? Everything was a lie, every smile hid a bored yawn; every promise hid a curse.

To make matters worse, one day a small, red-faced man came to the house explaining that he came from a Monsieur Vinçart of Rouen. He politely handed her a paper. It was a bill for seven hundred francs, signed by her. Lheureux had sold her bills to a money-lender! She sent the servant to fetch him. He was busy and could not come, and the stranger asked what reply he should take to Monsieur Vinçart.

'Well,' said Emma, 'tell him I haven't got it . . . It will have to be next week. Ask him to wait . . . Yes, next week, tell him.'

The man left without another word.

Next day, at twelve o'clock, a legal document was handed to her, and the sight of the piece of paper with the government stamp on it, and the name 'Maître* Hareng, Bailiff at Buchy,' written on it in big letters, scared her so much that she ran without a moment's delay to Monsieur Lheureux's shop.

She found him there, tying up a big parcel.

'What can we do for Madame today?' he asked, and he showed Madame upstairs to his little office.

'What's the matter?' said Lheureux, seating himself in his big armchair.

'Look at that.' And she showed him the paper.

'Well, what can I do?'

This made her more angry than frightened. Hadn't he promised not to sell her bills? He agreed that he had but added, 'I had no choice. I had a knife at my throat.'

'What's going to happen now?'

'Oh, I'll tell you what will happen; that's easy. You go before the judge, you pay or they sell your things. It's quite simple.'

Though Emma wanted to hit him, she asked him sweetly if there was anything she could do to keep this Vinçart quiet.

'Oh, no! Keep Vinçart quiet! You don't know much about him, that's clear. He's more bloodthirsty than a tiger!'

Emma cried out that Monsieur Lheureux really would have to do something.

---

* Maître: a French title given to lawyers.

'I think I've been pretty good to you! Look at this,' he said, opening a record book and running his finger up the page. 'Here . . . and again, here . . . 3 August, two hundred francs . . . 17 June, a hundred and fifty . . . 23 March, forty-six. In April . . .' He stopped. 'Anyway, I've had enough of these delays, and that's that!'

Emma said no more. What could she do?

When she went to Rouen, Léon gave her little comfort. He had just heard that he was going to be promoted to chief clerk in his law firm. It was time for him to think about his future. No more love-making! Besides, it rather bored him now when Emma began weeping on his chest, and he had grown tired of so much emotion. Feeling him withdraw from her, she now began to wonder how she could get rid of him! She even began to wish that something terrible would happen which would force them to separate. She stopped her excuse of music lessons, and her visits to Rouen. She stayed in her room, too depressed to pay attention when more legal demands for money came to the house, too depressed to talk to her husband or her child. She would have liked to stop living or else to go on sleeping for ever.

However, she could not stop the world coming to her, and one morning, two weeks after the first visit by Vinçart's man, Félicité brought her a piece of grey-coloured paper. She took it and read the complicated legal language which told her the simple truth that within twenty-four hours she had to pay the total amount of eight thousand francs. Lower down, she read the words which told her that if she did not do this, all her household goods would be sold! What could she do? Twenty-four hours! That meant tomorrow. Maybe Lheureux was just trying to frighten her, that's what it was! She went to see him.

'Do you know what's happening?' she said. 'I suppose it's a joke.'

'It isn't.'

'What do you mean?'

He turned to her slowly and then, folding his arms, said, 'Did you think, my little lady, that I would keep on supplying you with goods and money for ever, simply for the love of it? Be fair! I must recover my money one way or the other. Anyway, it's not me, it's Vinçart.'

'Couldn't you possibly. . . ?'

'I can't do anything.'

'But . . . just look at it like this . . .' And she began to say she had not known . . . it had taken her by surprise . . .

She begged and prayed, she even put her white hand on Lheureux's knee.

'That's enough of that!' he shouted. 'Anyone would think you were trying to make love to me.'

'You horrible man!'

'Well, who's got a temper?' he said, with a laugh.

'I'll tell everyone what you've done. I'll tell my husband . . .'

'All right, but I don't think your husband will be very pleased when he understands what you've been doing!'

She fell back, as if someone had hit her in the face.

And then he went close up to her, saying sweetly, 'It's not very pleasant, I know. But, after all, it never killed anybody, and it seems that it's the only way to make you pay me back my money . . .'

'But where can I get it?' said Emma.

'What about all those friends of yours?'

And he gave her a look so searching and so terrible that she shook with fear.

'I promise you,' she said. 'I'll sign any . . .'

'I've had enough of you and your signatures!'

'And I can still sell . . .'

'Don't be a fool,' he said. 'You've got nothing left to sell!'

'But if I brought you three thousand francs, a quarter, a third, nearly all of it?'

'No, it's no good.'

He pushed her gently towards the stairs.

'I beg you, Monsieur Lheureux, give me a few days longer!' and she burst into tears.

'Oh look, more tears!'

'But I'm desperate!'

'I don't care,' he whispered in her ear, so close she could smell his sour breath, and then he shut the door.

Chapter 15   A Death

She was brave next day, when Maître Hareng, the bailiff, accompanied by two witnesses, came to make a list of the goods to be sold. They began with Charles's consulting room, then went into the kitchen and bedroom. They examined her dresses, they searched through her dressing room – and her whole way of life, with all its little secrets, was laid bare, like a body on an operating table.

Maître Hareng, with his black coat buttoned up to the neck, his white tie and polished boots, would say from time to time, 'Pardon me, Madame; will you allow me?' And he frequently made little comments, such as, 'Charming! Very pretty!' Then he would make some more notes.

When they had gone through the rooms, they went up to the room under the roof. She had a desk up there in which she kept Rodolphe's letters. That had to be opened.

'Ah, letters!' said Maître Hareng, smiling politely. 'But allow me. I must make sure the box contains nothing else.'

At last they went and Félicité returned. Emma had sent her to look out for Charles and keep him away.

Charles that evening seemed rather worried. She looked at him, then at the curtains, the chairs, all the things which had made her a little happier, but which would now ruin them.

The next day, Emma went to Rouen to see if she could find a way out. She visited every banker she knew the name of. Some of them laughed in her face when they heard her story. All of them refused. At two o'clock, she ran to Léon's office. She knocked at the door, but no one came. At last Léon himself appeared.

'I've something I must say to you,' she said. She was very pale. 'Léon,' she said, 'I want you to do something for me.' Then, taking him with her two hands and giving him a shake, she said, 'Listen, I want eight thousand francs.'

'What? You're mad!'

'Not yet.'

And she told the story of what had happened, how she had let Lheureux lead her into disaster. And Charles knew nothing. She must have the money.

'How do you expect me . . .?'

And her lover would do nothing to help her. She had nowhere to turn to.

'What must be must be!' she said to herself.

She was woken at nine the next morning by voices in the square. There was a crowd of people outside, all trying to read a big piece of paper stuck to the wall of her house.

'Madame! Madame!' cried Félicité, rushing in. 'It's a terrible shame!'

And the poor girl held out a yellow paper which she had just torn off the front door. Emma read that all her furniture was to be sold. They looked at each other in silence. Servant and mistress had no secrets from one another.

'If I were you, Madame,' sighed Félicité at last, 'I would go and see Monsieur Guillaumin.'

'You would?'

'Yes, you go. That's the right thing to do.'

She dressed and, in order not to be seen (there were always a lot of people in the square), she took the path by the river.

'Monsieur,' she said, after she was let into the lawyer's dining room, 'I want to ask you . . .' And she told him her situation.

Maître Guillaumin knew all about it. In fact, he was a secret friend of Lheureux's, and knew the story better than she did herself. As he listened, he smiled a strange smile. When she asked him for help with the money that was being demanded, he said how sad he was that she had never come to him before. Then he put out his hand and took hold of hers, and kissed it greedily, playing with her fingers and looking in her face with his colourless eyes. She felt his breath on her cheek and could not bear it.

She jumped to her feet. 'Monsieur,' she said, 'I am waiting.'

'What for?' said the lawyer, suddenly going as white as a sheet.

'This money.'

'But . . .'

Then, giving in to a desire he could not resist, he said, 'Very well, yes! You can have your money!'

And he dragged himself along on his knees towards her, shouting, 'For God's sake, stay! I love you!'

He took her by the waist. Madame Bovary fell back with a terrible expression on her face, crying, 'I know I have fallen, Monsieur, but I am not to be sold.' And she turned and ran from the house.

Félicité was waiting for her on the doorstep.

'Well?' she asked.

'No!' said Emma.

And for the next quarter of an hour they went together through the names of all the people in Yonville who might perhaps help her. But every time Félicité mentioned a name Emma answered, 'Do you really think so? Oh, no, I'm sure they wouldn't.'

'And the Doctor will be here in a minute or two.'

'Yes, I know that . . . Leave me alone.'

Rodolphe! She had to see Rodolphe. He would help her, but

what should she say, how should she begin? Emma entered the park by the side gate, and walked to the house. She climbed the stairs and went to his room. He was sitting in front of the fire, with his feet up on the fireplace, just lighting a pipe.

'Hello! Is that you?' he said, getting up quickly.

'Yes, it's me. Rodolphe, I want to ask your advice.'

'You haven't changed, you are as charming as ever.'

'Ah,' she answered bitterly, 'sad charms. You said goodbye to them easily enough! Oh, Rodolphe!' she sighed. 'If you only knew . . . I loved you so!'

'You've been crying!' he said. 'Why is that?'

Now she began to weep uncontrollably. 'I am ruined, Rodolphe! I want you to lend me three thousand francs.'

'But . . . but . . .'

Hurrying over her words, she told him her story, to which he listened carefully. When she had finished, he looked sadly at her and replied, very calmly, 'I haven't got it, dear lady.'

It was no lie. If he had had it, he would have given it to her.

She stood for a few minutes looking at him.

'You haven't got it? Haven't got it?'

She repeated it several times, then she went out.

The walls seemed to be shaking, and she felt that the ceiling would fall on her. When she was outside, she felt a little better, but all her memories, all her ideas seemed to fill her head and burst in a single flash. She felt she was going mad.

Night was falling, and dark birds were flying into the trees. The sky seemed full of balls of fire, falling slowly to earth, turning and turning. What could she do? How could she face the world? She went running down the hill, through the market place and into the pharmacist's shop. The door was open and no one was there, though she could hear Justin, the assistant, talking to Monsieur Homais.

She entered the passage where the laboratory door was. On

the wall hung a key labelled 'Room 6'. It turned in the lock, and she went straight over and reached up to the third shelf, knocking over a small bowl which had stood beside it.

'Is anyone there? Who is that?'

She could hear Justin walking down the corridor. She must be quicker. She read the labels, her eyes desperately searching for one particular bottle, a bottle which might give her a way out of this impossible situation.

'Is there anyone there?'

She took down a blue jar with a small, hand-written label on it, pulled off the lid, and pushed her hand inside. She took it out full of a white powder which she began to eat then and there.

Justin ran into the room.

'Stop!' cried the boy, terrified, throwing himself on her.

'Be quiet, they'll come! They will blame your master for not locking his room.'

Then she left. They could do nothing to her now, and she felt a great peace in her heart.

Charles had come back to the house just after Emma left it to find Rodolphe. He did not know what to do. He sent Félicité to the Homais', the Tuvaches', Lheureux's, the Lion d'Or, everywhere. Whenever anxiety for his wife lifted for a moment, he saw his own life ruined, his money gone, Berthe's future destroyed. How? Why? Not a word. He waited until six o'clock in the evening. Then, unable to stand it any longer, he went out along the road for a couple of kilometres, saw no one, waited, and then came back again.

She had come home.

'What was the matter? Why? Tell me all about it.'

She sat down at her desk and wrote a letter, which she slowly closed, adding the date and the hour. Then she said, 'You will read that tomorrow. Until then, I beg you, do not ask me a single question . . . No, not one!'

'But...'

'Oh, leave me!'

And she lay down on her bed and seemed to fall asleep. She felt a bitter taste in her mouth, and it woke her up. She caught sight of Charles, and shut her eyes again. She tried to keep awake, wondering whether she had any pain. But no, nothing yet. She could hear the clock, the sound of the fire. Charles was standing by the bed, and she heard the sound of his breathing.

'Ah, it's nothing very much – dying!' she thought. 'I shall just fall asleep, and it will all be over.'

She drank some water and turned her face to the wall.

But there was still that horrible taste of ink in her mouth.

'I'm thirsty... oh, I'm so thirsty!' she sighed.

'What can it be?' said Charles, bringing her a glass of water.

'It's nothing... Open the window... I can't breathe.'

And she began to vomit so suddenly that she hardly had time to take her handkerchief from under her pillow.

He questioned her. She did not answer. She kept perfectly still, for fear the slightest movement would make her vomit again. And she began to feel an icy coldness rising from her feet to her heart.

'Ah, it's beginning now!' she whispered.

'What did you say?'

She kept moving her head gently from side to side, opening and shutting her jaws, as if she had something very heavy on her tongue. At eight o'clock the vomiting began again.

Charles, examining the basin, noticed something white at the bottom.

'That's extraordinary, most unusual!' he said.

'No, no, you're wrong,' she replied in a strong voice.

Then, very lightly, he passed his hand over her stomach. She gave a horrible scream. He stepped back, terrified.

Then she began to shake and became paler than the sheet that she was holding. Her heartbeat was irregular. There were drops of sweat on her face. Her eyes stared without seeing, and she answered every question with a shake of her head. She even smiled two or three times. Gradually her breathing became noisier. Then she started to scream.

'Oh, God, it's terrible!'

He threw himself on his knees at her bedside.

'Tell me! What have you eaten? For God's sake, speak!' And he looked at her with a tenderness in his eyes that she had never seen before.

'All right – over there . . . there!' she said weakly.

He ran to the writing-table, tore open the letter, and read aloud: 'Let no one be blamed . . .' He stopped, passed his hand across his eyes and then read on.

'What! . . . Help! Help me!' And all he could say was the word, 'Poisoned, poisoned!'

Félicité ran to Monsieur Homais' shop and he came back as soon as he heard what was the matter.

'Be calm,' said the pharmacist. 'What is the poison?'

Charles showed him the letter and the pharmacist realized there was little to be done.

Emma saw the two of them and looked at Charles.

'Don't cry,' she said, 'I will not be here to worry you much longer.'

'Why did you do it? Who made you do it?'

And she replied, 'It had to be, my dear.'

'Weren't you happy? Was it my fault? I did everything I could.'

'Yes, you did . . . You are kind, so kind.'

And she passed her fingers slowly through his hair.

'Bring the little one to me,' she said, raising herself on her elbow.

'The pain isn't getting any worse, is it?' asked Charles.

'No!'

The child came in, in her long nightdress. She looked thoughtful and not yet fully awake. She opened big, wondering eyes when she saw the room, and the bright candles.

'Oh, Mummy, how big your eyes are! How pale you are! And your face is all sweaty!'

Her mother was staring at her.

'I'm frightened,' cried the little one.

Emma took her hand and tried to kiss it; she struggled to free herself.

'That's enough! Take her away!' cried Charles.

After that Emma seemed a little better, but then she began to vomit blood, her limbs became stiff, her body was covered with brown patches, and her heartbeat raced. Then she began to scream again. She cursed the poison, she begged it to hurry up and finish its work. She pushed away everything that Charles tried to make her drink. He was standing stiffly by the bed, his whole body shaking from head to foot. Félicité ran from one end of the room to the other. There was nothing to be done except to call the priest.

When he came, Emma was lying with her chin sunk on her breast; her eyes were staring and her poor hands picked at the sheets. Pale as death, with eyes like burning coals, Charles – not crying now – was standing facing her at the foot of the bed, while the priest, resting on one knee, was whispering his prayers. Slowly she turned her head and suddenly, as she saw the priest kneeling beside her, a look of joy came over her face. The priest rose from his knees to show her the cross, and she leant forward and pressed her lips to the body of the Man-God. It was as if she kissed the figure on the cross with more love than she had ever given any person during her life.

She then fell back on to the bed, and they hurried to her side. Her life had ended.

Chapter 16   Endings

Death always comes as a shock, however much it has been expected. So when, at last, Charles saw her lying there so still, he threw himself on her, weeping.

'That's right,' said the pharmacist. 'Let nature have her way. You'll feel much better!'

Later, funeral arrangements had to be made. Charles thought carefully about these and wrote:

> I want her to be buried in her wedding dress, with white shoes and white flowers, and her hair loose over her shoulders. She should be covered with a large piece of green silk. These are my wishes. Make sure that they are carried out.

The gentlemen were surprised at Charles's ideas, and Monsieur Homais spoke to him.

'It seems to us,' he said, 'that silk is a little expensive . . .'

'That's none of your business!' shouted Charles. 'Leave me alone! You didn't love her, so just get out of my sight!'

That night, Charles, Homais and the priest sat beside Emma's body. She was lying with her head leaning over her right shoulder. The corner of her mouth, which was open, looked like a black hole at the bottom of her face; her two thumbs were held tightly in her hands. The sheet that covered her lay quite flat from her breasts down to her knees, rising up again at the tips of her toes, and it seemed to Charles as if an enormous weight was pressing down on her.

Early in the morning, Madame Bovary senior arrived. Charles, as he kissed her, again broke down and cried. Like the pharmacist, she criticized him about the funeral expenses, but he became so angry that she grew quiet.

Charles stayed by himself all afternoon. Berthe had been taken over to Madame Homais. In the evening, various people came in to see him and to express their regrets. He stood up and shook hands, but he could not say anything, and each newcomer sat down with the rest of the group, in a big circle round the fireplace. They all looked at the floor with serious expressions on their faces, and although everyone was bored, no one got up to go.

Upstairs Félicité, Madame Lefrançois and Madame Bovary senior were standing around Emma, busily finishing their task of dressing her.

'Oh, my poor mistress!' wept Félicité. 'My poor, poor mistress!'

'Just look at her!' said the landlady of the Lion d'Or. 'How pretty she looks even now!'

Then they all bent over to put the flowers on her hair. They had to lift her head a little, and as they did so, a stream of black liquid poured from her mouth.

'Oh, my God! The dress! Take care!' cried Madame Lefrançois.

Charles had to listen to the sound of hammers on wood as she was put into her last little home. Four men carried her to the door, the house was thrown open, and all the people of Yonville crowded near. Emma's father, Farmer Rouault, arrived as they were bringing her out, and fell unconscious in the market place when he saw the funeral carriage.

At the church Charles tried to think about the few times when they had been happy together – or when, at least, he had been happy with her. But remembering that she was there, underneath that green cloth, his heart was filled with black anger against God and against the world.

They sang, they went down on their knees, they got up again; there seemed to be no end to it all. He remembered how once, in the early days, they had gone to church together. They had sat on the other side, on the right, against the wall.

Outside the church Charles walked in front, holding himself very upright. Six men carried Emma's body, and the priest followed saying the prayers for the dead. His voice was carried over the fields, rising and falling on the wind. Sometimes a sudden turn in the path hid them from sight, but always the great silver cross rose high among the trees. The women followed, dressed in black, and each in her hand carried a tall lighted candle. Charles recognized every garden as he passed, and remembered how often, on mornings like this one, he had come away from one of them and set out for home and Emma.

Now they had arrived at the place where her grave had been dug. The people stood around, and all the time the priest was speaking, the red earth that had been piled beside the grave ran noiselessly down the slope into the dark hole. Then, when the four ropes were in position, they lowered her into the grave. Charles watched the wooden box go down until, at last, it arrived at the bottom and the ropes were pulled up again. The priest took the spade held out to him by his assistant and pushed the earth into the grave, then Charles sank down on his knees, throwing in handfuls of earth as he cried, 'Goodbye!' He sent her kisses, and dragged himself to the edge of the grave, wanting to lie with her.

They led him away, and he soon grew calm again, perhaps feeling, like all the others, a sense of relief that it was now all over. As the crowd walked back to the village, they talked about her death and what a terrible thing it was – especially Lheureux, who had made an effort to be there.

'Poor little lady! What a terrible thing for her husband!'

Emma's father insisted on going straight back to Les Bertaux, saying that he could not sleep in that house. He would not even see his little grandchild.

'No, no! I couldn't bear the pain of it. Goodbye, then. You're a good man,' and, pointing at his thigh, 'I shan't forget that leg, not as long as I live. You'll always get a bird from me at Christmas, don't you worry.'

When he reached the top of the hill he turned again, just as, years ago, he had turned and looked back along the Saint-Victor road when she had left him to go with her husband. The windows in the village were all on fire in the light of the evening sun. He put up his hand to shade his eyes and far away, on the horizon, he saw the place where she lay, with the trees, here and there, dark among the white stones. Then he went on his way.

Next day, Charles had Berthe brought home from the nurse. She asked for her mummy and they told her that she had gone away, that she would bring her back some toys. Berthe spoke of her again many times, but as the days went by she stopped thinking about her and Charles could not bear the child's happy laugh.

Life continued around Charles, but it had lost its meaning. When Madame Dupuis wrote to him to tell him of the 'marriage of her son, Monsieur Léon Dupuis, a lawyer in Yvetot, to Mademoiselle Léocadie Leboeuf, of Bondeville', Charles wrote: 'How delighted my poor wife would have been!', but he did not really care.

Besides, before long, his money troubles began again. Monsieur Lheureux's Vinçart returned once again with his demands. Now everyone tried to profit from Charles's loss. A music teacher in Rouen sent in a bill for six lessons, although Emma had never been to her once; a Madame Rollet demanded payment for delivering letters to Rouen. And day by day Charles had to sell the silver, piece by piece; then he got rid of the best furniture. All the rooms were robbed of their contents – except for one. Her room, her bedroom, was left as it had always been. When he had had his dinner, Charles went up there. He pulled the round table in front of the fire, moved her chair nearer, and then sat down facing it. A candle would be burning, and Berthe would be sitting near him, busy with her painting book.

Despite these efforts to keep Emma's memory alive, Bovary realized with sorrow that her face was fading from his memory. But every night he dreamed of her and it was always the same dream. He moved close to touch her, but just as he was taking her in his arms, she fell to dust.

And he was still in debt. Lheureux refused to wait any longer and Charles did not know what to do. At last, he decided he had to look in Emma's desk. There, instead of an answer to his problems, he found Léon's letters. He read them all, to the last line, then searched through every other piece of furniture, opening every drawer, emptying every box. In this way he also discovered a picture of Rodolphe – staring at him from a mountain of love letters.

Now people were shocked to see him so depressed. He never went out or had visitors; he even refused to go and see his patients. The only times he went out now were when he took his little girl by the hand, and they went together to the cemetery.

One day, when he had gone to the market at Argueil to sell his horse – his last possession – he met Rodolphe. They both turned pale. Rodolphe, who, when Emma died, had only sent his card, tried to give a few apologies. Then he grew braver, and invited Charles to have a bottle of beer with him at the inn. As they walked on, he talked about farming, the price of land, trying to avoid any uncomfortable subjects. Charles was not listening, Rodolphe noticed, and he anxiously watched his companion's face.

At last Charles said, 'I'm not angry with you.'

Rodolphe remained silent and Charles, with his head in his hands, repeated in a flat voice, a voice full of endless sorrow, 'No, I'm not angry with you now.' Then he said a great thing, the only great thing he had ever said: 'Fate is to blame!'

Rodolphe, who had controlled the direction of this particular fate for some time, thought this was rather a weak, even ridiculous response from a man in Bovary's position.

Next day, Charles went out and sat down on the seat in the garden. The sunlight came through the leaves, making shadows on the path, the perfume of the roses filled the air, the sky was blue, and bees flew from one open flower to the next. Charles felt disturbed, like a young man with an aching heart.

At seven o'clock little Berthe, who had not seen him that afternoon, came to fetch him in to dinner. His head was leaning back against the wall, his eyes were shut, his mouth was open, and his right hand was holding some long dark hair.

'Come on, daddy!' she said.

And, thinking he was only playing, she gave him a little push. He fell to the ground. He was dead.

When everything had been sold, just twelve francs remained, enough to pay for Mademoiselle Bovary's journey to her grandmother's house. That lady died the same year. As Farmer Rouault was by then too unwell to look after Berthe, she was taken in by an aunt. She is there still, but the aunt is poor and sends the little girl to earn her living in a cotton mill.

ACTIVITIES

Chapters 1–3

Before you read

1 Discuss these questions with another student. What do you think?

    a Would you call yourself a 'romantic' person? Why (not)?

    b What are the benefits and dangers of living a romantic life style?

    c What changes have there been in the legal position of women in your country over the last hundred years? What are some of the positive and negative effects of these changes?

2 Look at the Word List at the back of the book.

    a Find words for:

        – people   – things you can buy in a shop

    b Act out these feelings and expressions of emotion:

        blushing   feeling dizzy   feeling passion   shivering   sighing
        feeling terrified   weeping

While you read

3 Are these sentences about young Charles Bovary true (T) or false (F)?

    a He is a hard-working but untalented student.   .....

    b He receives a lot of help from his father.   .....

    c He falls in love with a 45-year-old widow.   .....

    d He meets Emma for the first time at her father's house.   .....

    e He blushes when Emma hands him his riding-whip.   .....

    f He is deceived by Heloise.   .....

    g His wife's death is good for business.   .....

    h He is confident that Emma will marry him.   .....

    i He is Père Rouault's idea of a perfect son-in-law.   .....

    j His mother enjoys the wedding.   .....

After you read

4 How do these people feel and why?

   a Charles's father, when he is 45 years old.

   b Emma, when she sees Charles for the first time.

   c Heloise, about Charles's visits to Les Bertaux.

   d Charles's father, when he investigates Heloise's financial affairs.

   e Charles, when Heloise dies.

   f Charles, after Emma talks to him about her mother.

   g Charles, when Père Rouault opens the front bedroom window.

   h Charles, on his wedding day.

   i Père Rouault, when Charles and Emma leave for Tostes.

5 Discuss these questions with another student.

Why

   a does Charles want to marry Emma?

   b does Emma agree to marry Charles?

   c is Père Rouault happy for Emma to marry Charles?

6 Work with another student. Have this conversation between Emma and her father. Are there any areas of agreement?

Student A: You are Emma. You prefer town life to country life. Tell your father why.

Student B: You are Père Rouault. You prefer country life to town life. Tell your daughter why.

Chapters 4–6

Before you read

7 Do you think Charles and Emma will be happy in their new life together? Why (not)?

While you read

8   Put these events in Emma's life in the correct order, 1–10.

   a   She throws away her wedding flowers.   .....

   b   She meets Léon.   .....

   c   She receives an unexpected invitation.   .....

   d   She moves into her new home in Yonville.   .....

   e   She reads Walter Scott novels.   .....

   f   She moves into Charles's house.   .....

   g   She spends a night in a château.   .....

   h   She loses her dog.   .....

   i   She loses interest in music and art.   .....

   j   She dismisses a maid.   .....

After you read

9   How does Emma feel about these people or things? Why?

   a   books

   b   the view from her bedroom window

   c   Djali

   d   dinner at La Vaubyessard

   e   dancing at La Vaubyessard

   f   life after La Vaubyessard

   g   Charles, as he gets older

   h   her wedding flowers

   i   the journey to Yonville

   j   the meal at the inn in Yonville

10   How does Charles feel about these things? Why?

   a   his early married life

   b   the theatre

   c   the evening at La Vaubyessard

   d   breakfast at La Vaubyessard

   e   Nastasie's dismissal

   f   Emma's home improvements

   g   professional ambition

   h   Emma's depression

   i   leaving Tostes

   j   the journey to Yonville

11 Work with another student. Have this conversation between Charles and a friend in Tostes.

> *Student A:* You are Charles's friend. You think that Charles is a good husband but has made some mistakes. Tell him what they are. How can he improve his relationship with Emma?
>
> *Student B:* You are Charles. You are worried about Emma, and you want advice, but you do not agree with your friend's criticisms of you. Tell him why.

Chapters 7–9

Before you read

12 In the nineteenth century, what problems would a couple like Léon and Emma face if they began a relationship? Would they face similar problems today, in your country? Why (not)?

While you read

13 Tick (✓) the correct answer.
  a Monsieur Homais is
  - a qualified pharmacist.   .....
  - disliked by the authorities.   .....
  - unpopular in Yonville.   .....

  b The Bovarys give their daughter
  - the name of Charles's mother.   .....
  - an Italian name.   .....
  - the name of a stranger.   .....

  c Emma becomes a more dutiful wife because she
  - is afraid of her true feelings.   .....
  - is worried about her daughter.   .....
  - feels calmer about life.   .....

  d Léon wants to leave Yonville because he feels
  - guilty.   .....
  - jealous.   .....
  - bored.   .....

    e Monsieur Boulanger is
- sensitive and experienced. .....
- intelligent and romantic. .....
- cold-hearted and selfish. .....

After you read

14 How does Emma feel about these people or things, and why?
    a her husband's work
    b her husband's behaviour when she is pregnant
    c the birth of her child
    d Léon's presence in the wet nurse's house
    e Léon, after the visit to the mill
    f life with Charles, after her visit to the mill
    g Léon's departure for Paris
    h spitting blood
    i the speeches at the Agricultural Show

15 How are these important in this part of the story?
    a card games
    b Emma's sudden interest in church and children
    c Charles sitting happily by a fire
    d dizziness

16 Discuss these questions with another student. What do you think?
    a Is Emma a good mother? Why (not)?
    b Is Léon right not to tell Emma his true feelings? Why (not)?
    c What advice would you give Emma about Rodolphe ? Why?

Chapters 10–12

Before you read

17 Chapter 10 is called 'Presents for a Lover'. In your opinion, what are suitable presents for lovers? Who do you think is going to give presents in this story?

18 Who or what are these sentences about?

    a Charles thinks that it will be good for
       Emma's health. ....

    b Emma and Rodolphe become lovers there. ....

    c Emma and Rodolphe meet regularly there
       during the winter. ....

    d Emma hides it from Charles. ....

    e Emma dreams of going there with Rodolphe. ....

    f It affects Emma's health. ....

    g Charles tries not to think about them. ....

    h Emma has it destroyed. ....

    i Emma has to explain it to Charles. ....

    j Emma meets him in Rouen. ....

After you read

19 What role do these play in the relationship between Emma and
Rodolphe?

    a hunting

    b Charles

    c a garden wall

    d Charles's work

    e Emma's delicate emotions

    f a riding whip

    g Monsieur Derozerays

    h Emma's daughter

    i Lheureux

    j lies

20 What role do these play in the relationship between Emma and
Léon?

    a Monsieur Homais

    b Charles

    c *Lucia di Lammermoor*

    d a glass of water

    e the singer's qualities

    f Léon's experience in Paris

g a letter

h the cathedral

i a carriage

21 In Chapter 12 Flaubert writes, 'she intended to keep her distance, to be responsible.' Why does Emma have this intention? Why does she nevertheless become Léon's lover? Discuss these questions with another student.

Chapters 13–16

Before you read

22 Discuss these questions.

    a How do you think the story will end for:

        Emma?   Charles?

    b How do you think the story *should* end for each of them?

While you read

23 Which of these sentences about Emma are true (T)?

    a She shares Charles's grief over his father's death.   .....

    b She manages Charles's financial affairs.   .....

    c She visits a lawyer's office in Rouen.   .....

    d She improves her piano skills.   .....

    e Léon loses interest in her.   .....

    f She refuses M. Guillaumin's offer of help.   .....

    g Rodolphe lends her money.   .....

    h Père Rouault blames Charles for her death.   .....

    i Charles learns about her love affairs after her death.   .....

    j Her daughter now works on a farm.   .....

After you read

24 How does Emma feel about these people before she dies? Why?

    a Lheureux

    b Léon

    c Monsieur Vinçart

    d Maître Hareng

    e Félicité

    f Charles

25 Who says these things, who to, and why?

   a 'Oh, it's nothing! The night air is a little cool.'

   b 'You should never let a natural gift lie unused.'

   c 'He's more bloodthirsty than a tiger!'

   d 'It seems that it's the only way to make you pay me back my money.'

   e 'I know I have fallen, but I am not to be sold.'

   f 'They will blame your master for not locking this room.'

   g 'It's beginning now!'

   h 'Was it my fault?'

   i 'I couldn't bear the pain of it.'

   j 'I'm not angry with you.'

26 Discuss these questions with another student.

   a Find eight ways in which Emma deceives Charles in this part of the story.

   b How does Charles discover the truth about Emma's affairs?

   c Why does Léon lose interest in Emma?

   d Would the end of the story be different if Emma had accepted Maître Guillaumin's proposal? Why (not)?

   e Do you feel sorry for Emma at the end of the story? Why (not)?

Writing

27 Imagine that you are Emma (Chapter 2). Write a page in your diary for a day some time after your father broke his leg. Describe daily life on the farm, your feelings about Charles Bovary and your hopes for the future.

28 Imagine that you are Emma (Chapter 5). Write a page in your diary some time after your marriage. Describe a day in your life in Tostes, and your life with Charles.

29 Imagine that you are Monsieur Homais. You want to sell your pharmacy. Write an advertisement for a pharmacy magazine, describing the wonderful opportunities that your business would provide and the attraction of life in Yonville.

30 Imagine that you are Charles's father. You hear that Emma is unhappy with life with Charles in Tostes and wants to move. Write a letter to her, telling her why she is being unfair on Charles and why moving is a bad idea for your son's career.

31 Imagine that you are Rodolphe (Chapter 9). Describe in your diary your feelings about Emma and her husband after your first meeting.

32 Imagine that you are Charles (Chapter 11). Write a letter to your father, asking for help and advice. Explain your worries about Emma and the reasons that you think lie behind your financial situation.

33 Imagine that you are Léon (Chapter 14). Write a letter to Emma from Rouen, explaining why you cannot see her again.

34 Imagine that you are a local journalist. Write a report for your newspaper on the tragic deaths of Dr Bovary and his wife.

35 'If Charles had been a more sensitive husband, the tragedy would not have occurred.' Do you agree with this statement? Why (not)?

36 Charles says about the tragedy, 'Fate is to blame!' Do you agree with him? Why (not)? Write your essay, using events from the story to support your view.

Answers for the Activities in this book are available from the Penguin Readers website. A free Activity Worksheet is also available from the website. Activity Worksheets are part of the Penguin Teacher Support Programme, which also includes Progress Tests and Graded Reader Guidelines. For more information, please visit:
www.penguinreaders.com.

WORD LIST

bailiff (n) someone whose job is to take the property of people who owe money

blush (n/v) to become red in the face, usually because you are embarrassed

breeze (n) a light, gentle wind

cemetery (n) a place where dead people are buried

champagne (n) a French wine with bubbles that is often drunk on special occasions

cherry (n) a small, round, soft red fruit with a large seed

cider (n) an alcoholic drink made from apples

cigar (n) a thick roll of dried tobacco leaves, which people smoke

convent (n) a place where a group of religious women live and work

dizzy (adj) feeling that you are losing your balance, perhaps because you are ill or have turned around too quickly

draper (n) someone who sells cloth, articles for dress-making, and sometimes clothing and other things made of cloth

dressing-gown (n) a piece of clothing like a long, loose coat that you wear before you get dressed

fate (n) a power that is believed to control what happens in people's lives; the things, usually bad or serious, that happen to someone

franc (n) old French money, which is not in use now

maid (n) a female servant

mistress (n) the female employer of a servant; the female owner of a dog

passion (n) a very strong feeling, usually of love or of belief in something

pharmacy (n) a shop where medicines are prepared or sold

practice (n) the work of a doctor; the place where a doctor works

shiver (v) to shake slightly because you are cold or frightened

sigh (n/v) a heavy breath out, especially when you are tired or annoyed

statue (n) a stone, metal or wooden object that has been made to look like a person or animal

stockings (n pl) a pair of very thin pieces of clothing that fit closely over a woman's feet and legs

sunset (n) the time when the sun disappears and night begins

terrified (adj) very frightened

textile (n) material or cloth

viscount (n) the title of an upper-class man

vomit (v) to be sick, so that food comes back up from your stomach and out of your mouth

weep (v) to cry

wet nurse (n) a woman who is hired to breast-feed someone else's child